A Taste of Mey
Recipes and Memories
Inspired by the Castle of Mey, Caithness
Home of Her Majesty Queen Elizabeth The Queen Mother

First published in 2011
by The Queen Elizabeth Castle of Mey Trust
The Castle of Mey
Thurso
Caithness
Scotland
UK
KW14 8XH

Email: enquiries@castleofmey.org.uk
www.castleofmey.org.uk

ISBN: 978-0-9569604-0-5

A CIP catalogue record of this is available from the British Library

Designed by Iain MacLeod-Jones
www.imjdesign.co.uk

Printed by St Andrews Press of Wells, Somerset

A Taste of Mey

Recipes and Memories

Inspired by the Castle of Mey, Caithness
Home of Her Majesty Queen Elizabeth The Queen Mother

Foreword by

HRH The Prince Charles, Duke of Rothesay

Compiled & Edited by
Christina Murray

contents

introduction

"I wait with impatience for August to come round each year, when I can once more look out under these wide skies over the Pentland Firth, or enjoy the distant view to the South, to Morven and the Sutherland hills. Caithness means so much to me."

From a speech made by Her Majesty Queen Elizabeth The Queen Mother in August 1990, on receiving a 90th birthday present from Her friends in Caithness.

A Taste of Mey began as a 'light supper by the fire', only over time to become a magnificent 'banquet' of marvellous memories and tempting food. It was not a 'magic' transformation though, and this splendid result is the outcome of many people's efforts associated with the Castle of Mey and Her Majesty Queen Elizabeth The Queen Mother, the Castle's proud owner for nearly fifty years. It is a story of great affection for an inspiring person and as well as for a unique place, which for so long was a haven for Queen Elizabeth and Her many friends who visited. The Castle of Mey remains to this day a vibrant, welcoming destination for countless people still to appreciate and enjoy, which is a fitting tribute to Queen Elizabeth who saw its potential as a wonderful home.

So push open the big oak front doors of the Castle of Mey and come inside with us to join the party. Here is your chance to share and savour this unique collection of anecdotes and favourite recipes connected with Queen Elizabeth. You will not go hungry and *A Taste of Mey*, with its myriad stories, recipes and stunning photographs, will be your guide.

There are recipes from Oeufs Drumkilbo, and the Roast Saddle of Mey Selections Lamb served at the wedding of The Duke and Duchess of Cambridge, to the famous Jam Puffs and a Royal Clootie Dumpling from Stornoway. You will catch snippets of conversations too, which will give you a fascinating insight into the life of Her Majesty Queen Elizabeth The Queen Mother, as well as those who have contributed. It is an occasion rich in friendship, fun and loyalty and one not to be missed!

"I have enclosed some of my recipes and a couple of my anecdotes forever in my memory and my heart, as Mey simply does that."

From a contributor

Christina Murray
Editor

Queen Elizabeth welcomes the Duke of Rothesay at Scrabster Harbour

I am more than delighted to have acted as President of The Queen Elizabeth Castle of Mey Trust since it was established as an independent Scottish charity, with great foresight, by my dearly beloved Grandmother, The Queen Mother, in June 1996. The Trust's aim remains to ensure that The Castle of Mey in Caithness is preserved as a living entity in order to provide employment in a very remote area of these isles, whilst offering an educational benefit to the wider public in a variety of different spheres.

The Castle of Mey is not an imposing building and thanks to the sympathetic way in which the trustees have orchestrated the transition from the only home which my Grandmother ever owned to a major tourist attraction in the north of Scotland, it retains its unique atmosphere and is often described by visitors as 'homely'. Every year, in August, I am fortunate enough to be able to stay in the Castle and I have fallen in love with it and the local area. However, maintaining such an ancient building in such a remote and exposed location is no easy task and consumes a great deal of capital and effort. Determined to raise funds for the Castle, those working at Mey decided to put together a collection of recipes and memories within this splendid book as a tribute to Her Majesty and her Northern home. I am most grateful to all the contributors and sponsors, but special thanks are due to Christina Murray, the wife of the Administrator, who has overseen this whole project.

My Grandmother's friends, members of Her Household, past and present employees of the Trust, and Patrons and Friends of The Castle of Mey, have combined to produce this charming and, I hope, appetizing book, which I hope will find a place on coffee tables as well as in kitchens throughout the land. It provides a number of insights into a remarkable life, whilst containing a selection of favourite recipes – many of which I have adored since childhood.

I do hope that you will enjoy 'A Taste of Mey', secure in the knowledge that in buying a copy you will have helped to maintain a much-loved home of Her Majesty Queen Elizabeth The Queen Mother, for future generations to enjoy.

acknowledgements

For a book with so many strands, my thanks to everyone involved with *A Taste of Mey* are many.

Initially the idea of a Castle of Mey recipe book was that of Shirley Farquhar, at the time Manager of the Castle of Mey Visitor Centre. She envisaged a small spiral-bound collection to be sold in the Castle shop and persuaded me to be the Editor.

We had not, however, reckoned with Iain Ball, a Patron of the Castle of Mey, offering to pay for the book's design, which transformed *A Taste of Mey* from its quiet beginnings into a larger and rather up-market publication. To say we are grateful to Iain Ball is putting it mildly, and I would like to thank him enormously for all his support in the successful completion of this marvellous project. I would also like to thank his wife Helen for the fantastic hospitality which she has given me on my visits to Somerset. It is very evident that Iain MacLeod-Jones is most talented both as a photographer, and as the designer of *A Taste of Mey*. I would like to thank him greatly for so many hours of sympathetic collaboration and some extremely funny moments, as we have felt our way through unknown but such rewarding territory.

I am not sure that it is in the remit of the Chairman of The Queen Elizabeth Castle of Mey Trust to help in the creation of a recipe book, but I am very grateful to Ashe Windham who has been wonderfully supportive to me, 'opening doors', guiding me through 'do's and don'ts', as well as providing some fantastic recipes.

There would not have been *A Taste of Mey* without the many contributors who have so willingly given their recipes and memories and I am incredibly grateful to them all for their help. They have risen superbly to the occasion and made *A Taste of Mey* unique and very special.

We have gathered a wonderful supporting cast and the following are to be thanked most sincerely for their help. Nancy McCarthy and Helen Malcolm for cooking delicious cakes for photoshoots in the Castle and making things look 'as they were', Iain Malcolm for his stalwart help moving furniture and props, and Beatrice Farmer for the extra work *A Taste of Mey* has made in the office. Lance Purcell for cooking so willingly and perfectly the recipes photographed in the Castle Visitor Centre, and Annie Stewart from ANTA in Tain, Ross-shire, for very generously giving us a fantastic selection of their Queen Mother Check stoneware and fabric for the photos.

I would also like to thank Clare Macpherson-Grant Russell of Ballindalloch Castle and *I Love Food* fame for a marvellous afternoon of help and advice, and Michael Sealey and Sue Simpson for such help in the reconstruction of 'A Royal Dinner' and the many favourite recipes of Queen Elizabeth.

Finally, on a personal note, I must thank James, my husband, who as always has been a wise and wonderful rock, as have been our most dear three daughters and their families.

Christina Murray
Editor

We would like to thank Mr Jeremy Goring, Chief Executive of The Goring Hotel, London,
for his enormous generosity in sponsoring The Queen Elizabeth Castle of Mey Trust
to hold their annual drinks party and fundraising event at the Goring.
It was, of course, Her Majesty's favourite London hotel.

❧

We also wish to acknowledge, with sincere thanks, the following Patrons of the Castle of Mey who,
along with others, most generously donated towards the publishing of
A Taste of Mey at the Goring Drinks Party, May 2011:

❧

The Hon. Mrs Acloque
Sirdar Aly Aziz
Patric & Ann Baird
Lady Louise and Anthony Burrell
His Honour Judge & Mrs Simon Coltart
Peter Cooper
Charles and Bridget Galbraith
The Jordan Foundation
Julia Hunt-Grubbe
Mr George King – remembering his mother Mrs Audrey Bannerman
Lady Lever of Manchester
Leonara Countess of Lichfield
Mr William Lorimer – in memory of his beloved cousin Amanda Caroline Severne of Shakenhurst
Mrs Petra Platt
Graham & Jean Pugh
Mr John Rank
Mr Alan Ross
David Sinclair
Mr Jim Stobo CBE DL
Dick Turpin FIH
Amanda Ward
Mr & Mrs Philip Watson
Mrs Hilary M Weston CM O.Ont.
Ashe Windham CVO

contributors

Lady Elizabeth Anson	*Niece of Queen Elizabeth*
Mrs Ann Baird	*Patron of the Castle of Mey*
Prebendary Helen Ball OBE	*Patron of the Castle of Mey*
Mrs Emma Bartlett	*Daughter of the Editor*
Mr Henry Bellingham MP	*MP for NW Norfolk*
Mr John Bowes-Lyon	*Cousin of Queen Elizabeth*
Mrs Gillian Brockway	*Friend of the Castle of Mey*
Earl of Caithness PC	*Trustee of The Queen Elizabeth Castle of Mey Trust*
Mrs Gwen Coghill	*Shop Manager at the Castle of Mey Visitor Centre*
Mr John Collings RVM Bar	*Head Chauffeur to Queen Elizabeth*
Mrs Sue Collings RVM	*Chef to Queen Elizabeth*
Mrs Felicity Colville	*Friend of the Castle of Mey and volunteer Castle of Mey Guide*
The Countess of Dalhousie	*Brechin Castle*
Captain William de Rouet MVO	*Equerry to Queen Elizabeth*
Mrs Sarah Jane Drumbrille	*Friend of the Castle of Mey – Ontario*
Miss Anne Dunnett JP	*Lord-Lieutenant of Caithness*
Lady Edmonstone	*Friend of the Castle of Mey*
Lady Elworthy	*Friend of the Castle of Mey*
Mrs Sheila Farley-Sutton	*Friend of the Castle of Mey*
Mrs Hazel Farquhar	*Member of Castle of Mey Staff*
Mrs Naomi Featherstone	*Niece of William Tallon, Page of the Back Stairs to Queen Elizabeth*
Mrs Delia Findlay	*Friend of the Castle of Mey*
Miss Fiona Fletcher CVO	*Lady Clerk to Queen Elizabeth*
Mr Henry Gillespie	*Friend of the Castle of Mey*
Mrs Carol Gilmour	*Friend of the Castle of Mey*
Lady Gilmour	*Friend of the Castle of Mey*
Mrs Jenny Gordon-Lennox LVO	*Lady-in-Waiting to Queen Elizabeth and now to HM The Queen*
Mr Roly Grimshaw LVO MBE	*Equerry to Queen Elizabeth*
Mr Bruce Guest	*Footman to Queen Elizabeth*
Mrs Bunty Gunn	*Friend of the Castle of Mey*
Mrs Sheila Heggie Main	*Friend of the Castle of Mey*
Mrs Barbara Hiddleston	*Castle of Mey Archivist*
Mrs Day Howden	*Castle of Mey Gardening Consultant*
Mr Clive Illingworth	*Friend of the Castle of Mey*
Mrs Marjorie Isgar MBE	*Friend of the Castle of Mey*

Mrs Sue Jenkins	*Friend of the Castle of Mey*
Lt Col. Richard Jenkins LVO TD	*Equerry to Queen Elizabeth*
Mrs Jackie Johnstone	*Castle of Mey Guide*
Mrs Catriona Leslie LVO	*Lady-in-Waiting to Queen Elizabeth*
Mrs Susan MacColl	*Friend of the Castle of Mey*
Mrs Catherine MacKenzie	*Friend of the Castle of Mey*
Mrs Margaret MacKenzie	*Friend of the Castle of Mey*
Mrs Etta Macleod	*Friend of the Castle of Mey and fundraiser for Macmillan Nurses*
Mrs Clare Macpherson-Grant Russell	*Friend of the Castle of Mey and Lady Laird of Ballindalloch Castle*
Major Malcolm Macrae	*Friend of the Castle of Mey and 12th Laird of Breckness Orkney*
Mrs Judith Maddocks	*Friend of the Castle of Mey*
Mrs Pat Maguire	*Friend of the Castle of Mey*
Mrs Helen Malcolm	*Daily Lady and Castle of Mey Guide*
Mr Andrew Manson	*Head Chef at Mackays Hotel, Wick*
Mrs Nancy McCarthy	*Senior Daily Lady and Castle of Mey Guide*
Major David McMicking LVO	*Equerry to Queen Elizabeth*
Mr Norman McMullen KstG	*Friend of the Castle of Mey – Ontario*
Mrs Joan Miller	*Castle of Mey Website Editor*
Miss Alice Murray	*Daughter of the Editor*
Mrs Christina Murray	*Editor of A Taste of Mey*
Mr Edward Murray	*Chef, and nephew of the Editor*
Lt Col. James Murray DL	*Castle of Mey Administrator*
Mrs Susan Murray	*Friend of the Castle of Mey, Lucknam Park Hotel and Spa*
The Hon. Mrs Nicolson	*Friend of the Castle of Mey*
Mr Mike Palmer	*Friend of the Castle of Mey*
Ms Lili Panagi	*Patron of Castle of Mey*
Lady Penn LVO	*Lady-in-Waiting to Queen Elizabeth*
Major John Perkins DL	*Friend of the Castle of Mey and occasional Castle of Mey Guide*
Major-General Jeremy Phipps	*Friend of the Castle of Mey*
Mrs Susan Phipps	*Friend of the Castle of Mey and, as Susan Crawford, leading Equestrian artist*
Mrs Olga Polizzi	*Internationally renowned hotelier and wife of William Shawcross*
Lady Poole	*Friend of the Castle of Mey*
Mr Hamish Pottinger	*Friend of the Castle of Mey*
Mr Lance Purcell	*Chef at the Castle of Mey Visitor Centre*
Mr Derek Quelch	*Executive Chef at The Goring Hotel*

15

Major-General Sir Sebastian Roberts KCVO OBE	*Former Colonel of the Irish Guards*
Mrs Hilary Robertson	*Supervisor of the Castle of Mey Visitor Centre Tearoom*
Mr Kenneth Rose CBE	*Historian and author*
Mr Michael Sealey RVM(Gold)	*Head Chef to Queen Elizabeth*
Mr David Shaw	*The Schoolhouse Restaurant, John O'Groats*
Mr William Shawcross CVO	*Friend of the Castle of Mey and official biographer of Queen Elizabeth*
Mrs Christine Shearer	*Friend of the Castle of Mey and volunteer Castle of Mey Guide*
Mrs Ruby Sinclair	*Friend of the Castle of Mey and former volunteer Castle of Mey Guide*
Mrs Clare Steen	*Daughter of the Editor*
Mrs Wilma Stewart	*Shop assistant in the Castle of Mey Visitor Centre*
Mr Jim Stobo CBE DL	*Former Trustee of The Queen Elizabeth Castle of Mey Trust*
The Dowager Countess of Strathmore	*Widow of Fergus 17th Earl of Strathmore, nephew of Queen Elizabeth*
Margaret Viscountess Thurso	*Friend of the Castle of Mey*
Mr Alan Titchmarsh MBE DL	*Honorary Patron of the Friends of the Castle of Mey*
Mr Dick Turpin FIH	*Patron of the Castle of Mey and former consultant to the Castle of Mey Visitor Centre*
Mr Hugo Vickers DL	*Friend of the Castle of Mey and writer and broadcaster*
Miss Jane Walker-Okeover LVO DL	*Extra Woman of the Bedchamber to Queen Elizabeth*
Mrs Betty Watson	*Wife of former Keeper at Glenmazeran, latterly the estate of Lord Elphinstone*
Mrs June Webster RVM	*Retired Housekeeper at the Castle of Mey*
Mr Julian Williams	*Formerly Head Chef to TRHs The Duke and Duchess of Rothesay*
Mrs Arabella Windham	*Interior designer and artist*
Mr Ashe Windham CVO	*Chairman of The Queen Elizabeth Castle of Mey Trust, Equerry to Queen Elizabeth and Extra Equerry to HRH The Prince of Wales*

A Note from the Editor

The very nature of this book is that it contains many people's favourite recipes and each has a 'voice'. It is our hope that you will enjoy browsing and using the recipes, and that in the process of trying to standardise the format of the recipes so that they are easy to follow, we have not lost their individuality. We would ask you to give us the benefit of the doubt, in some instances, as to how many people the recipes are for, the generality of the instructions and on occasions slightly imprecise quantities. As with being given any recipe by a friend, a small amount of personal judgement and suiting of your individual needs is required!

a Royal dinner...

Demie-Hemard Froid
..
Filet de Boeuf Rôti.
..
Salade
..
Le Gratin de Pêches
Crème Chantilly
.

Dimanche Le 28 Septembre

Dinner with Queen Elizabeth The Queen Mother

This menu card is on display in the Dining Room at the Castle of Mey. It was written by Michael Sealey RVM (Gold), Queen Elizabeth The Queen Mother's Head Chef for forty years, for a dinner party held by Her Majesty on Sunday 28 September 1980. Chef cooked for the occasion and he has now very kindly recreated the recipes which you will find over the next few pages.

Chilled Lobster Halves
with a Dill Mayonnaise

~

Roast Fillet of Beef
with Yorkshire Puddings and Horseradish Sauce

~

Salad

~

Peach Gratin
with Chantilly Cream

demi homard froid

chilled lobster halves with a dill mayonnaise

SERVES 6
1 cold cooked lobster (approx. 1.5 lb/675g)
1 round leaf lettuce
½ pint/300ml mayonnaise (homemade or bought)
1 dessertspoon chopped fresh dill or ½ teaspoon anchovy essence or 1 teaspoon tomato purée
6 slices brown bread and butter

Chop the lobster in half lengthways and remove the meat from the tail and claws and set aside. Discard the entrails from the centre of the lobster.

Replace and arrange the claw and tail meat into the empty shell.

Wash and dry the lettuce and arrange with the lobster on a platter.

Mix the mayonnaise and dill (or other seasoning) and serve in a sauce boat alongside the lobster and brown bread and butter.

The seating plan used by Her Majesty Queen Elizabeth, still in the Dining Room at the Castle

filet de boeuf rôti

SERVES 6
1½ lb/675g fillet of beef (at room temperature)

For the Yorkshire puddings
4 oz/100g plain flour
8 floz/230ml whole milk
1 egg
½ teaspoon salt
¼ teaspoon white pepper

For the gravy
½ pint/300ml beef stock (homemade or tinned)
1 teaspoon arrowroot powder
2 tablespoons cold water

For the horseradish sauce
4 ozs/100g hot horseradish sauce
4 flozs/150ml whipped cream

Heat a little oil in a roasting pan until very hot. Sear the beef on all sides until brown (about 2 minutes per side). Place in a preheated oven at 180°C/375°F/Gas 4 (reduce temperature by 10°C/50°F if using a fan oven) for medium rare 20 minutes per lb/450g, well done 35 minutes per lb/450g (approximately). Remove from the oven and cover with foil and leave to rest in a warm place prior to serving.

For the Yorkshire puddings, place the flour, salt and pepper in a bowl. Make a well in the centre and add the egg. Mix together and gradually add the milk. Whisk until it reaches the consistency of double cream. Strain through a sieve to remove any lumps and allow the mixture to rest for at least an hour in a cool place before cooking. Preheat the oven to 180°C/375°F/Gas 4. Oil a Yorkshire pudding or muffin tin and place the oiled tin in the oven. Heat the oil until it is very hot. Remove the tin from the oven and carefully put a ladleful of Yorkshire pudding mixture into each well of the tin. Quickly return the tin to the oven and cook for 35 minutes. Check their progress through the glass in the oven door – try not to open the door at least in the first half of cooking or they will sink. Once cooked remove the tin from the oven and arrange the puddings on a platter.

For the horseradish sauce, whip the cream until soft peaks form. Place the horseradish sauce in a bowl, add the cream and fold it in gently. Serve in a sauce boat. For the gravy, having removed the beef from the roasting tin after the resting time, heat the tin on the cooker and add the stock to deglaze the tin, capturing all the delicious juices and crispy bits into the liquid. Add the arrowroot powder to the cold water and mix until the lumps are gone. Gradually add this mixture to the gravy, whisking all the time. Simmer gently for 2 minutes until thickened. Serve in a sauce boat.

To serve the meal, thinly slice the beef, arrange on a warmed platter and moisten with a little gravy. Serve with the Yorkshire puddings, horseradish sauce and gravy. Accompany with seasonal vegetables and/or salad.

The Dining Room at Castle of Mey including Queen Elizabeth's champagne glass (opposite top right)

gratin de pêche
served with a chantilly cream

SERVES 6
6 ripe yellow-flesh peaches
½ pint/300ml medium white wine
4 oz/100g caster sugar
4 medium egg yolks

Blanch and peel the peaches before cutting them into halves (or quarters depending on size) and place in a shallow ovenproof dish. Pour over the wine, sprinkle with the sugar and leave to marinate for at least one hour in a warm place (about body heat, 37°C/99°F, is ideal).

Just before serving, drain the marinade into a bowl, add the egg yolks and whisk together over a pan of simmering water (bain-marie) until thickened and a ribbon like consistency is achieved. Do not heat too much or stop whisking – you will get alcoholic scrambled eggs!

Pour the marinade over the peaches and place under a hot grill until golden brown.

Serve with whipped cream, slightly flavoured with brandy (if desired).

Cordial Congratulations
on the exquisite
Gratin de Pêches

ER

A complimentary message to Chef from Queen Elizabeth

to start

The kitchen scales at Castle of Mey

lady loyd's twice-baked soufflés

SERVES 8-12

5 oz/125g spinach leaves
2½ oz/70g butter
3 oz/75g freshly grated Gruyère cheese
3 oz/75g grated Parmesan
¾ pint/400ml (or a little less) whole milk

2 oz/50g flour
4 large eggs, separated
Just less than ¾ pint/400ml double cream, seasoned
Salt, pepper and freshly grated nutmeg

Ramekins at Mey

Butter ramekin dishes (8 large or 12 small) with butter from the allowance. Shred the spinach finely, put in a pan with the milk, bring to the boil, stir and set aside. To make a white sauce, mix the remaining butter with the flour and then add the milk and spinach and cook until thick and smooth. Beat in salt, pepper, nutmeg, Gruyère and then the egg yolks. Whisk the egg whites until they form stiff peaks and then fold into the cheese mixture.

Spoon the mixture into ramekins arranged in a deep baking tin, with boiling water halfway up the sides of the dishes. Cook in a preheated oven at 200°C/400°F/Gas 6 for 15 to 20 minutes. Allow to cool for about 15 minutes and then turn out of the ramekins (the soufflés can be frozen at this point until needed; defrost and follow remaining instructions) and arrange in a shallow ovenproof dish, buttered and sprinkled with half the grated Parmesan. Pour the seasoned cream over the soufflés, sprinkle with remaining Parmesan and bake at 200°C/400°F/Gas 6 for 15 to 20 minutes or until well risen. Serve at once.

Catriona Leslie

kippastatta

"*Both Jeremy and I have had many happy times with Queen Elizabeth, particularly at Birkhall, and it was here one year that I was especially touched by Her Majesty. We were walking in the garden, chatting and stopped by a Rosemary bush. "Ah," She said, "Rosemary for remembrance". To which I replied, "Well, Ma'am I certainly won't need that to remember You by!" and on we went. Later, I went upstairs to change for dinner, and there on my dressing table was a dear little crystal vase with a sprig of rosemary in it, tied up with ribbon.*"

6-8 kipper fillets
Vinaigrette dressing made with balsamic vinegar
2-4 leeks
½ onion
Ground black pepper

Prepare the day before you need it (always a help). Remove the skin from the fillets, and cut the flesh into smallish pieces. Place in a flat dish and marinate the fish in the dressing.
Chop and cook the leeks, then drain well. Cut the onion into very thin slices, separate the rings and scatter on top of the fish. Arrange the leeks round the edge of the dish and season with black pepper before serving with toast and butter.

Susan Phipps

hara shorva
a gently spiced cream of pea soup

" Delicate and delicious! I often double up the quantities and freeze some. "

SERVES 5-6 (makes 2½ pints/1.5 litres)

4 oz/100g peeled and diced potato
3 oz/75g onion peeled and chopped
2 pints/1 litre chicken stock
¾ in/2cm cube fresh ginger, peeled
1 teaspoon ground coriander seeds
2 teaspoons ground cumin seeds
5 tablespoons chopped fresh coriander or parsley

½ fresh hot green chilli
10 oz/275g shelled peas (fresh or frozen)
¾ teaspoon salt
1 tablespoon lemon juice
½ teaspoon ground roasted cumin seeds
¼ pint/150ml double cream

Combine potato, onion, chicken stock, ginger, ground coriander and ground cumin in a pot and bring to the boil. Cover and reduce the heat to low and simmer for 30 minutes.

Fish out the cube of ginger and discard. Add the fresh coriander, chilli, peas, lemon juice, roasted cumin and salt. Bring back to boil and simmer, uncovered for 2 to 3 minutes or until peas are just tender.

Empty into an electric blender in batches and blend until smooth. Put into a clean pan, add cream and bring to a simmer to heat through.

Ruby Sinclair

curried courgette soup

SERVES 4-6

6 courgettes, chopped
2 medium onions, chopped
2½ pints/2 litres chicken stock
1 tablespoon medium curry powder
1 tablespoon flour
2 tablespoons oil

Heat the oil and gently cook the onions. Add the curry powder and flour and a little stock to help the roux. Cook for 1 minute. Add the courgettes and the rest of the stock. Simmer for 10 minutes, then liquidise and check the seasoning. Serve adding a little single cream for a touch of luxury.

Bunty Gunn

curried sweet potato soup
white beans add texture

2.2 lb/1 kg orange-fleshed sweet potatoes
2 pints/1.2 litres boiling water or stock
Sea salt and pepper
14 oz/400g tinned white beans
1 teaspoon good curry powder
2 tablespoons chopped fresh parsley or coriander leaves

Peel the sweet potatoes and cut into small cubes. Add the boiling water or stock, sea salt and pepper, and bring to the boil. Simmer for 15 minutes or until the sweet potato is soft. Drain the beans and rinse. Add half the beans and the curry powder, stirring well then whiz in a food processor in batches, being careful not to overfill the bowl. Return to the pan, add the remaining whole beans, and heat gently. If it is too thick, add extra boiling water. Taste for salt, pepper and curry powder, and scatter with the parsley or coriander.

The Dowager Countess of Strathmore

35

cullen skink
a classic Scottish dish made with smoked haddock

SERVES 4
2 large undyed smoked haddock fillets
1 large onion peeled and chopped
2 large potatoes peeled and chopped
1 oz/25g butter
16 floz/450ml milk

Poach the haddock in a pan with 10 floz/300ml water and the butter for approximately 20 minutes. Remove the fish and add the potatoes and onions with some pepper. Cook until the vegetables are tender.

Remove from the heat and mash roughly. Add the milk and fish and reheat gently.

Serve with Scottish oatcakes.

Lance Purcell

This thick soup originates from the Scottish village of Cullen in Morayshire. Lance buys his smoked haddock from Colin at McKays the Fishmonger in Thurso, who used to supply The Queen Mother with fish when She was at the Castle of Mey.

A bowl of cullen skink, freshly prepared in the Vistor Centre Tearoom by Lance Purcell

lunchtime soup

1 large onion, finely chopped
1 large leek, finely chopped
3 sticks celery, diced
3 carrots, diced
2 tins chopped tomatoes
1 oz/25g butter

1 tablespoon tomato purée
3 handfuls pasta shells
3 bay leaves
3 pints/900ml beef (or venison) stock
Parmesan cheese

Sauté the onion and leek in the butter until transparent. Add the diced carrots and celery and season with salt and pepper. Cook for a few minutes then add tomato purée, bay leaves and stock. Bring to the boil then add the pasta shells. Cook until the pasta is 'al dente'.

Sprinkle with grated Parmesan and serve with garlic bread or Red Onion and Pepper Focaccia (see recipe on page 135).

Delia Findlay

leek and cucumber soup

" *This recipe is so easy and is usually well received. If anybody asks me what the ingredients are I tend to say mixed vegetables rather than mention cucumber!* "

SERVES 4-6

1 tablespoon oil
1 desertspoon butter
1 large cucumber (remove skin if preferred)
1 leek

1 large onion
1 pint/600ml chicken stock
Small tin evaporated milk
Fresh parsley, chopped

Melt oil and butter over a low heat. Add roughly chopped vegetables, and sweat without browning for 15 minutes. Add chicken stock and simmer for a further 20 minutes. Blend with an electric hand blender or sieve for a smoother finish. Just before serving, add the evaporated milk and parsley without bringing back to boil.

Margaret MacKenzie

pear and parsnip soup

an unusual but delicious combination

SERVES 6
1 oz/25g butter
12 oz/350g parsnips, chopped
1 onion, chopped
2 large conference pears, peeled, cored and chopped
1 pint/600ml chicken stock
½ pint/300ml milk
Salt and pepper
Chopped fresh parsley, to garnish

Melt the butter in a large saucepan. Add the parsnips, onion and pears. Fry gently until the onion is transparent.

Add the stock and milk and bring slowly to the boil. Season with salt and pepper, cover and simmer gently for approximately 20 to 30 minutes, or until the vegetables are tender.

Puree the soup and check the seasoning. Garnish with the chopped parsley and serve with oven baked-croutons or crusty bread.

This unusual combination makes a deliciously warming soup for a cold day.

Etta Macleod

The Tastes of a Queen

Queen Elizabeth's tastes in food were simple and traditional; they perhaps derived from the food She ate as a child at Glamis Castle.

Her Majesty loved haddock and other simple fish like sole. Her chef served Her monkfish once and never again, She said. She insisted that fruit and vegetables be in season and preferably English. She thought Spanish strawberries tasted like turnips. Queen Elizabeth loved omelettes and disliked smoked salmon, oysters, coconuts and capers.

In the latter part of Her life, Her chef was Michael Sealey and She used to send him little notes, praising some dishes fulsomely and making suggestions for the next day's menus.

In Scotland, nothing gave Her more pleasure than picnics and they happened almost every day, rain, snow or shine. Again the food was simple, but fun, especially the jam puff and cream pastries which would explode all over the faces of the uninitiated. Indeed, fun was encouraged at all meals, as in other parts of Her life. And to create the right atmosphere, a glass of something was always welcome – gin and Dubonnet on picnics, Champagne on many other occasions.

In the 1930s She created a secret society at court. They called themselves "The Windsor Wets" and many years later She explained, "The great thing was that being a SECRET SOCIETY we had to have a secret sign, and this was to raise the glass to other members without being seen by the disapprovers." Such conviviality remained with Her all Her life.

William Shawcross

Opposite, above: Glamis Castle, the childhood home of Queen Elizabeth
Opposite, below: On one of Her Majesty's many picnics (from L to R: Dennis Dawnay; Her Majesty; Commander Clare Vyner RN; Sir Martin Gilliatt; Lady Doris Vyner; Captain David McMicking; Ruth, Lady Fermoy).
Photograph courtesy of Captain Richard Jenkins (who was taking the photograph, hence the empty chair!)

asparagus mousse

" Makes a good light lunch or supper dish. "

1 large tin of asparagus
1 large tub cream cheese
½ oz/12g gelatine dissolved in 2 tablespoons of liquid from asparagus tin
¼ pint/150ml cream
2 egg whites, whipped stiff

Blend all the ingredients together except egg whites. Fold in the egg whites last and put in the fridge to set.

Jane Walker-Okeover

mushroom paté

1 onion, chopped
½ lb/225g mushrooms, chopped
1 oz/25g breadcrumbs
3 oz/75g butter
3 rashers of bacon

4 oz/100g cream cheese
Squeeze of lemon juice
Brandy (optional)
Salt and pepper

Grill the bacon until crisp; drain, cool and chop. Cook the onion gently in oil until soft. Add the mushrooms and cook gently over low heat for 2 to 3 minutes. Stir in the breadcrumbs. Liquidise the mixture along with the bacon, cheese, butter, salt and pepper, and lemon juice to taste. Add brandy, if desired. Best left in fridge for a day to mellow.

Christine Shearer

petits royales au parmesan
consommé is the secret ingredient

SERVES 4

2 eggs, plus 3 egg yolks
½ pint/300ml consommé
1 level dessertspoon chopped fresh parsley or chervil
1 level dessertspoon chopped fresh chives
1 level teaspoon powdered thyme or oregano
¼ pint/150ml double cream
1 oz/25g grated Parmesan cheese
1-2oz/25-50g grated Gruyère or Emmental cheese

Beat the eggs and egg yolks together. Bring consommé to boil over a low heat, together with the herbs. Simmer uncovered for 5 minutes. If time is scarce it is not absolutely necessary to simmer the consommé with the herbs. Gradually strain the consommé into the eggs, stirring all the time. Blend in 2 tablespoons of the cream.

Butter four ramekin dishes and pour in the consommé mixture. Set them in a roasting tin containing ½ in/1¼cm of water, and cover dishes with buttered greaseproof paper. Bake in centre of a pre-heated oven at 180°C/350°F/Gas 4 for about 15 minutes or until set. Remove and leave to cool before chilling in the fridge for a few hours.

About 20 minutes before serving pre-heat oven to 200°C/400°F/Gas 6. Unmould the ramekins into a buttered ovenproof dish and pour over the remaining cream. Cover with the Parmesan and sprinkle generously with the Gruyère or Emmental cheese. Place the dish near the top of the oven and bake until the cheese melts and turns golden. Serve at once with brown buttered bread and finely chopped watercress sandwiches.

Christina Murray

a simple chicken liver paté
with smoked bacon, garlic... and cream crackers

1 lb/450g chicken livers
½ lb/225g smoked bacon
13 oz/325g butter
3 or 4 cream crackers

1 egg
1 crushed clove garlic
Black pepper
Sea salt (I prefer Maldon)

" Perhaps my paté would have been a little too robust for Queen Elizabeth's table, where every dish seemed to exude or conceal cream. The late Lord Arran used to say, 'No need to put your teeth in when lunching at Clarence House'! "

Lightly fry chicken livers in 10oz of the butter so that they are brown outside and pink within. Put the fried livers and uncooked bacon through a mincer. (A blender makes the mixture too smooth.)

Put the minced livers and bacon into an oven dish with a lid together with any melted butter and juices from the frying pan. Break up the cream crackers to the size of crumbs and add to the mixture together with the crushed garlic, pepper and salt. Add the egg and stir the mixture thoroughly with a fork so that all the ingredients are evenly distributed. Cover the dish with greaseproof paper or foil, put on the lid and cook in a preheated low oven (150°C/300°F/Gas 2) for about 1 hour.

Remove the dish from the oven and pour away the melted bacon fat surrounding the paté. Melt the rest of the butter in a pan and pour over the paté. Allow to cool and serve slightly chilled with hot crisp toast. The paté should be moist and its inside pink.

Kenneth Rose

oeufs drumkilbo
a legendary favourite

His Royal Highness The Prince Charles, Duke of Rothesay has suggested that this recipe should be included as it was such a favourite of Her Majesty Queen Elizabeth The Queen Mother. It is a great favourite with the Royal Family and its fame has taken it into the cookery sections of both the *Daily Telegraph* and *The Spectator* too.

David Morgan Hewitt, the Managing Director of The Goring Hotel, which The Queen Mother visited regularly, says, "Oeufs Drumkilbo is really like a posh prawn cocktail and egg mayonnaise all wrapped into one. We still serve it on our menu each day with fond memories of Queen Elizabeth's many visits to The Goring, and it remains a firm favourite with our guests today".

Here is the definitive answer to the origins of Oeufs Drumkilbo which, in its telling, had become rather like a Chinese Whisper. I am told by the Dowager Lady Elphinstone that it was created by Mrs Cruikshank, the 17th Lord Elphinstone's first cook at Drumkilbo (pictured), where they lived in the early 1950s. This recipe is from Julian Williams, formerly Head Chef to Their Royal Highnesses The Duke and Duchess of Rothesay, which was adapted from a recipe given to him by Michael Sealey RVM (Gold), Queen Elizabeth The Queen Mother's Head Chef for forty years.

Christina Murray

SERVES 6-8

¾ pint/450ml mayonnaise
4 diced hard boiled eggs
8 oz/225g prawns (cooked but chilled fresh or frozen)
8 oz/225g diced lobster (cooked but chilled fresh)
3 diced ripe tomatoes (blanched, skinned and de-seeded)
1 dessertspoon anchovy essence
6 drops Tabasco sauce
1 dessertspoon tomato purée
4 sheets leaf gelatine or 2 oz aspic jelly crystals
¼ pint/150 ml warm fish stock

Soak the leaf gelatine in cold water then dissolve it in the fish stock and allow to cool OR dissolve the aspic jelly crystals in the warm fish stock and allow to cool. Place the mayonnaise in a bowl and add half the cooled gelatine or aspic mixture. Add all the other ingredients to the mayonnaise mixture and stir carefully to combine. Place the mixture in a china or glass bowl and chill until set.

Glaze with the remaining gelatine or aspic and decorate at will and allow to set. Serve with fingers of brown bread, mustard and cress.

cucumber creams

a light savoury summer treat

" We had such a delightful day in March 1986 when The Queen Mother invested me, Marjorie Isgar, with my MBE for services to education. We consequently became Friends of The Castle of Mey in order to support the Castle, even though we knew we would be unable to visit because of the distance involved. "

SERVES 6-8

1 block of lime jelly cubes
1 teaspoon salt
6 floz/175ml boiling water
2 tablespoons white vinegar
1 teaspoon grated onion

6 flozs/175ml crème fraîche or soured cream
3 floz/75ml mayonnaise or salad cream
1 cucumber, minced and drained
Salad leaves to serve
Freshly ground pepper

Dissolve the jelly and salt in the boiling water and then stir in the vinegar and onion. Sprinkle on the pepper and chill until beginning to thicken. Mix in the crème fraîche, mayonnaise or salad cream, and cucumber. Pour into individual shaped moulds and allow to set. To serve, arrange the salad leaves on plates and place the unmoulded cucumber creams in the centre. This recipe can also accompany the Salmon Paté (see page 52) to make a more substantial starter or lunch dish.

Marjorie Isgar and Pat Maguire

smoked fish paté

8 oz/225g smoked fish
4 oz/100g softened butter
Small onion (finely chopped)

3 oz/75g cream cheese
1 teaspoon curry powder
Salt and pepper

Skin, bone and flake fish. Put the fish, cheese, half the butter, curry powder, onion and seasoning in a bowl and beat together. Spoon into ramekin dishes and smooth the tops. Melt the remaining butter and drizzle over the tops. Garnish with slices of lemon and serve chilled with fingers of toast.

Christine Shearer

PARTY PLANNERS
LADY ELIZABETH ANSON
56 LADBROKE GROVE LONDON W11 2PB lea@party-planners.co.uk
TELEPHONE: 020 7229 9666   FACSIMILE: 020 7727 6001

Lobster, Crayfish or Crab Entrée

(A recipe from Lady Glamis, the sister-in-law of Queen Elizabeth and my Great Aunt by marriage.)

Cut the flesh into small discs. To every two tablespoons of fish take one tablespoon of white sauce and one of cream. Add salt and cayenne to taste and one teaspoon of grated parmesan. Mix up well and put into fire-proof dish. Put a few breadcrumbs on top, sprinkle with parmesan and small pieces of butter and bake in a hot oven for ten minutes.

Egg Pancakes

(A recipe from Glamis Castle adapted by my mother, Her Highness Princess Anne of Denmark.)

8-10 thin, unsweetened pancakes   Three-quarters of a pint/450ml of béchamel sauce
3 hardboiled eggs   Strong meat gravy

Chop eggs fairly finely and add béchamel sauce & a dessertspoon of grated parmesan cheese. Put a spoonful on each pancake & roll up. Heat on a plate over hot water. Just before serving pour over a little reduced meat gravy. Serve grated parmesan cheese separately.

the starter from seville

SERVES 4

2 grapefruit
2 avocado pears
9 oz/250g prawns
4 hard-boiled eggs
Fresh parsley to garnish, chopped

For the sauce

4 tablespoons mayonnaise
2 teaspoons Tabasco sauce
1 tablespoons tomato purée
1 tablespoon tomato ketchup

Remove all the skin and pith from the grapefruit and segment. Skin and slice the avocados into similar segments. Cut the hard-boiled eggs lengthways and segment also. Arrange the ingredients in a 'clock face' style around each plate - avocado next to grapefruit, next to hard-boiled egg, next to prawns. Mix all the sauce ingredients together and put a spoonful in the centre of each plate and garnish with chopped parsley. Serve with slices of good, wholemeal bread and unsalted butter.

Bunty Gunn

Mey time in the Equerry's Room

pork terrine

" Good to take on the hill or to the river in a bap! "

1 lb/450g pork belly
1 lb/450g pork (or venison) liver
1 lb/450g bacon lardons
1 packet thin streaky bacon
2 bay leaves

Line a 2 lb/1kg loaf tin with streaky bacon. Put in bay leaves. Put pork belly in a food processor until minced. Add bacon bits. Process again, then add liver with some salt and pepper and process again until just mixed. Pour into loaf tin.

Place the loaf tin in a larger tin and fill with water until it is halfway up the sides. Place in moderate oven (180°C/350°F/Gas 4) for 1½ to 1¾ hours or until skewer comes out clean. Allow to cool with a weight on top. Turn out and serve with salad or crusty bread.

Delia Findlay

pear, stilton and walnut salad
simple but delicious

SERVES 6
I bag of lettuce – lamb's lettuce is good
2 ripe pears
6 oz/150g good quality stilton
6 oz/150g packet of halved walnuts
Some salad dressing

Arrange a covering of lettuce on each plate. Crush the walnuts and sprinkle over the lettuce, then crumble or cube the stilton and add on top. Peel and cut the pear into slithers and place these on the salad. Finally pour a small amount of dressing on to each salad (or just a little balsamic and olive oil). The stilton and walnuts can be crumbled and crushed in advance but the assembling of the salad and peeling of the pear is best left to the end.

Arabella Windham

smoked salmon surprise

8 oz/250g smoked salmon
4 tablespoons taramasalata
2-3 tablespoons crème fraîche
4 oz/100g king prawns (cooked and peeled)

Line four ramekin dishes with cling film and then with strips of smoked salmon, draping both over the sides – leave enough hanging to fold over and cover the top. Mix 4 tablespoons of taramasalata with 2 tablespoons of crème fraîche. Put a spoonful of this into each ramekin, add two or three prawns and cover with another spoonful of the mixture. Pull up the slices of smoked salmon and cover the tops of the ramekins. Draw up the cling film and cover also. Place in the fridge until ready to be served. Turn out on to a plate (the cling film makes this quite easy), garnish with salad leaves or rocket, any spare prawns and a wedge of lemon.

Bunty Gunn

salmon paté
combine with cucumber creams if you're hungry

SERVES 4
4 salmon fillets
12 oz/300g soft cheese
3 tablespoons crème fraîche
1 tablespoon chopped fresh chives
1 tablespoon lemon juice
Salt and pepper

Fry, grill or poach the fillets and then allow to cool before flaking them. Mix the other ingredients together then gently stir in the flaked fish. Line four ramekins with cling film and divide the paté equally between them. Chill in the fridge for a couple of hours before unmoulding and serving. This recipe can accompany the Cucumber Creams (see page 48) to make a more substantial starter or lunch dish.

Marjorie Isgar and Pat Maguire

A salmon in the Library

meat

Casseroled Lamb Chops with Mushrooms
made by Lance Purcell (see recipe on page 58)

roast saddle of Mey Selections lamb

" This saddle of Mey Selections lamb was served at the wedding of The Duke and Duchess of Cambridge on 29 April 2011. "

SERVES 6

1 saddle of lamb (ask your butcher for lamb
  saddle off the bone)
½ oz/10g finely chopped fresh rosemary
1 lb/500g spinach
Pinch of sea salt and freshly ground black pepper
24 fresh asparagus spears
24 young carrots
12 baby leeks
2 lb/lkg Jersey Royal potatoes
Small bunch of flat parsley
2 oz/50g unsalted butter

For the jus

6 lb/3kg lamb bones
4 onions
1 lb/500g carrots
1 head of celery
1 lb/500g leeks
6 bay leaves
Bouquet garni of rosemary and thyme
Arrowroot (if desired)
Redcurrant jelly (optional)
17½ floz/500ml red wine and 7 floz/200ml port

The stock for the jus needs to be made 24 hours in advance. Start with the lamb bones, roasting them at 200°C/400°F/Gas 6 for 30 minutes. Drain the fat and reserve for later. In the pot that will be used for the stock, brown off the vegetables on a high heat for 5 to 10 minutes with a little butter and salt, then add the bones, bay leaves and bouquet garni and cover with cold water. Skim any fat that rises to the surface before putting on the heat. Bring to the boil and simmer for 6 hours. Drain the stock through a fine sieve and refrigerate overnight.

In the morning, skim off the fat and reserve (ensure no stock is still attached to the fat). Reduce the stock by two thirds. In a separate pan, reduce the wine and port by two thirds or until it reaches a slightly more syrupy appearance, then combine with the reduced stock and thicken with a little arrowroot, if desired. Season to taste. If the jus is slightly bitter add a little redcurrant jelly to taste.

For the spinach, blanch it in boiling water for 10 seconds and refresh in iced water. Place the spinach in a towel and ring out, then place it in a bowl, add the rosemary and season to taste. Down the middle of the lamb saddle, in between the two cannons, evenly spread your spinach mixture then tie up tightly. Transfer to the fridge until ready for using.

For the vegetable garnish, trim the asparagus spears one third up from their bases then peel from the tips to the bottom using a vegetable peeler. Blanche for 2 minutes and refresh in iced water. Trim the root and tops of the leeks. If desired, take the first outer layer off. Blanche for 2½ to 3½ minutes or until al dente. For the young carrots, peel and leave 10mm of green shaw and trim the rest. Blanche for 2½ to 3½ minutes or until al dente. Slice the Jersey Royals in half lengthways, boil in salted water for 12 minutes or until tender, then drain and leave to cool. At this point everything is ready apart from the lamb; you are only 1 hour from the dish being complete.

Preheat the oven to 200°C/400°F/Gas 6. Season the lamb skin that will be the lovely crackling with salt and pepper, place in a roasting tin and cook for 30 to 40 minutes (depending both on how pink you like your lamb, and on the size of your saddle). Once the lamb is cooked allow it to rest in a warm place for the same amount of time it was cooked for before slicing and serving. As the lamb rests, warm the jus through (do not let it boil and reduce any more), warm the Jersey Royals in half butter, half lamb fat and finish with shredded flat parsley.

For reheating the rest of the vegetables, bring some butter in a hot pan past the foaming stage and onto a nut brown stage (beurre noisette), then add an equal quantity of lamb fat to stop the butter burning, immediately add the vegetables and allow them a couple of minutes to warm back through. Drain on kitchen paper. Bon appétit!

Andrew Manson
Head Chef at Mackays Hotel Wick, owned by Mr Murray Lamont.
Mr Lamont is also Chairman of North Highland Tourism.

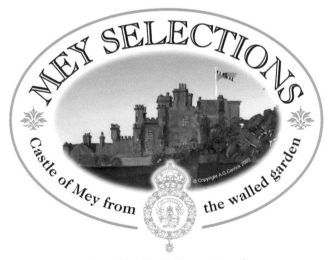

Mey Selections is an initiative of The Duke of Rothesay in the North Highlands of Scotland, where highest quality products are exclusively sourced, wherever possible, from within a hundred miles of the Castle of Mey.

Reproduced by kind permission of
His Royal Highness The Prince Charles,
Duke of Rothesay

casseroled lamb chops with mushrooms

❝ I thought it would be fun to give a recipe from my late husband Robin. Soon after he took his seat in the Lords, their Lordships were asked for their favourite recipes for a new book entitled 'Eat Like a Lord'. I looked up the recipe that Robin had produced and found it was for tripe. Actually it was a very good French recipe – 'Tripe a la Moche de Caen' with cider and calvados but, as my butcher confirmed, tripe is no longer allowed to be sold!

I remember Robin telling me that Queen Elizabeth had said to him one evening at dinner that She thought it was a pity mutton seemed to have gone out of fashion, and he resolved to put that right, with a gift of one of his sheep from the hills. This recipe does not mention mutton, but it was one that Robin loved to do on one of his ventures into the kitchen and which became a favourite. ❞

SERVES 4

4 best end neck of lamb chops	1 oz/25g butter
4 oz/100g button mushrooms	1½ oz/35g flour
2 tablespoons red currant jelly	¼ pint/150ml meat stock
1 tablespoon Worcestershire sauce	1 pinch nutmeg
1 tablespoon lemon juice	Ground black pepper and salt to taste

Trim the chops of excess fat. Heat the butter in a frying pan and brown chops quickly. Transfer chops to a casserole dish and put the washed mushrooms on top. Retain the fat in the pan. In a saucepan melt the redcurrant jelly slowly. Add the Worcestershire sauce, lemon juice, nutmeg and seasoning. Add the flour to the fat in the frying pan. Blend in the stock and the redcurrant mixture, then bring to the boil and simmer for 2 minutes. Pour over the chops and mushrooms. Cook in a very moderate oven (170°C/325°F/Gas 4) for 1¼ hours.

This dish can be put in the fridge overnight and reheated so that any fat can be removed if necessary.

(Recipe pictured on page 55)   **Margaret Viscountess Thurso**

ballindaloch mince and cheesey potato pie

SERVES 6-8

1 lb/450g minced Scotch beef
1 onion, chopped
2 tablespoons oil
Worcestershire and tomato sauces to taste
Seasoning
1 tablespoon plain flour
½ pint/300ml beef stock
Gravy browning (optional)
1 lb/450g lightly boiled potatoes, sliced

For the cheese sauce

1 oz/25g butter
1 oz/25g flour
½ pint/300ml milk
2 oz/50g grated strong cheese
1 egg yolk
Seasoning

Grated strong cheese (for topping)

For the cheese sauce, place butter, flour and milk in pan and whisk madly until thick. Add egg yolk and cheese, and season to taste.

Gently fry onion in oil. Sprinkle with flour and allow to colour. Add mince and cook over a gentle heat for 5 minutes. Add stock, sauces and seasoning to taste. Simmer, stirring occasionally, for 20 minutes. Pour into fireproof dish. Cool. Cover with the cheese sauce and then a layer of sliced potatoes. Sprinkle with some grated cheese and place in a fairly hot oven (180°C/350°F/Gas 4) for 15 minutes.

Clare Macpherson-Grant Russell

A statue of a prize-winning Angus bull

Castle of Mey gardens

mrs bell's moussaka

"*Mrs Bell was my Kew landlady and rescued me from my previous digs where wildlife roamed the mattresses! She was an arty soul, very Bloomsbury in her tastes and talents, and took me to concerts at the Royal Albert Hall, the Royal Festival Hall, St John's Smith Square and the like. She also insisted that I visit the National Portrait Gallery and the Wallace Collection in Manchester Square. As well as being a good painter and potter, she also wrote children's books about a character called Mrs Apple, who lived at 'the End Cottage'. I owe my artistic education to Eileen Bell and she was a good cook too, this moussaka being one of her own creations. I love it, rich and creamy with sultanas! It always reminds me of my time at the End Cottage by the Thames at Kew. Happy days.*"

SERVES 6

1lb/450g mince
1 onion, chopped
Chopped garlic to taste
Sultanas, handful
1 teaspoon dried or chopped fresh mixed herbs
Nutmeg, to taste
1 tablespoon brown sugar
1 glass red wine (optional)

Small tin tomatoes
Flour
Stock (optional)
Vinegar
½ lb/225g spaghetti, cooked
1 pint/600ml white sauce
Grated cheese

Fry mince with all above except cheese sauce and spaghetti. Thicken with flour and moisten with stock or water but leave quite firm. Put in a deepish pie dish. Make thick white sauce and grate cheese into it. To each ½ pint of sauce add 1 dessertspoon of vinegar with the cheese. Pour cheese sauce over the mince. Cook for 10 minutes at 180°C/350°F/Gas 4. Delicious!

Alan Titchmarsh

Alan Titchmarsh is the Honorary Patron of the Friends of the Castle of Mey and says that "the garden at the Castle of Mey is without a shadow of doubt my favourite Royal garden."

fillet steak with blue cheese and croutons

> **"** *A really special recipe for fillet steak and I am sure that Aberdeen Angus would be the best. I have used it many times over the years as a special treat for myself and my family.* **"**

SERVES 1
2 oz/50g blue cheese (my favourite is Irish Cashell Blue)
1 7-8oz/225g (1½ in/4cm thick) fillet steak
1 oz/25g butter
A few croutons
Salt and pepper
Watercress, to garnish

Season the steak with salt and pepper and seal on both sides in the butter in a very hot pan. Transfer to a buttered baking sheet (I use baking parchment on the baking sheet instead of butter) and then slice the cheese until you have enough to cover the fillet steak. Put into a very hot oven (220°C/425°F /Gas 7) for 5 minutes for rare, 8 minutes for medium rare (I like mine this way), or 15 minutes for well done, allowing the cheese to melt and lightly colour. Transfer the steak to a hot plate, scatter round the croutons and pour around the cooking juices. Garnish with a few sprigs of watercress and serve immediately with chips, peas and tomatoes.

Gillian Brockway

romanian-style baked pork chops
with peaches and paprika

SERVES 4

4 pork chops
4 level teaspoons gravy granules
Black pepper

5 oz/125g finely chopped onion
2 level teaspoons paprika
1 large tin sliced peaches

Sprinkle both sides of chops with gravy granules. Fry the onion in a little oil and add the pepper and paprika. Fry until pale gold. Put chops in oblong casserole dish and add the onions. Pour the juice of the peaches over the chops and add the peaches. Cover with lid or foil and cook for 1 hour at 180°C/350°F/Gas 4. Uncover for the last 15 minutes for chops to brown. Serve with mixed vegetables and mashed potatoes.

Hilary Robertson

hungarian pork fillet

1½ lb/600g pork fillet
2¼ lb/1.25kg potatoes
12 tablespoons lesco sauce (see recipe on page 130)

Cut the meat into twelve rounds and flatten with a mallet. Boil potatoes in their skins in salt water, drain, peel and cut into slices.

Fry the potato in oil and mix with the lesco. Heat through. Fry the meat in oil for three minutes each side and serve on top of the potato lesco mix. Serve with seasonal vegetables.

Ann Baird

savoury pancakes
make in advance and heat up later

SERVES 4 (makes about 8 pancakes)

For the filling
1 onion, chopped
8 rashers bacon, chopped
½ lb/225g mushrooms, chopped
1 tub crème fraîche
1 teaspoon wholegrain mustard
Mixed herbs (optional)

For the batter
4 oz/100g plain flour
1 egg, beaten
½ pint/300 ml milk

For the batter, place the flour in a large bowl, make a well in the centre and then gradually add the egg and milk, whisking continuously, until you have a smooth batter. Allow the batter to stand for 30 minutes.

For the filling, heat oil in a frying pan and add the onion until softened. Add the bacon and cook until crisp. Add the mushrooms and cook until soft. Add the crème fraîche, mustard and herbs, if desired, and cook until heated through.

Fill pancakes with the filling and arrange in greased ovenproof dish. Any spare filling can be put over top of pancakes.

Cook in a moderate oven until heated through. Serve with a green salad.

Marjorie Isgar and Pat Maguire

"Now, let's all pretend it's the War..."

Queen Elizabeth The Queen Mother was lunching with my husband and me in our house in Suffolk before attending a concert in the Maltings Concert Hall at Snape during the Aldeburgh Festival in the 1970s. It was a large party of about twelve people, including Benjamin Britten, Raymond Leppard and Sir Frederick Ashton.

The first course was an Avocado Mousse in a ring mould with mushrooms in the middle. We had a butler for the occasion who dropped the mousse as he came through the dining room door. There was a shocked silence. I quickly, and I hope calmly, went through to the kitchen to break the news to our infuriated cook who had heard the crash and was ready to murder the poor man. She produced a very small one which had been intended to feed Her Majesty's chauffeur and Her protection officer. The butler handed it to The Queen Mother who asked for a teaspoon and taking a very small helping indeed She said, "Now, let's all pretend it is the War, and we can only eat a tiny little piece each." The mousse went round the table and was unfinished. She managed to turn a domestic disaster into a most enjoyable game.

She never forgot it and reminded me of the occasion many times in the future.

Lady Penn

66

sunday lunch lamb casserole

"This dish sits happily in the bottom oven of the Aga for 2 to 2½ hours and cooks away while I am at Church. I can then invite people for lunch and do not have to worry! It is my adapted own invention and all I have to do is heat up the mashed potato and cook a vegetable. This is so useful."

SERVES 4
8 lamb cutlets
1 oz/25g butter
½ lb/225g peeled shallots or onions, chopped (I prefer shallots)
½ lb/225g tomatoes, chopped
1 carrot, sliced (optional)
Mixed herbs
Pinch of salt and a few peppercorns
Chopped fresh parsley

Melt the butter in a shallow casserole. Trim the excess fat off and add lamb cutlets, then turn them in the hot butter. Add the rest of the ingredients. Cover tightly. Cook in a slow oven (150°C/300°F/Gas 2). I have a two oven Aga and give it 10 minutes at the top and move it down (don't forget!) to the slow oven for 2 to 2 ½ hours. By some miracle it makes its own delicious gravy. I sprinkle some chopped parsley on top for eye appeal.

Best served with mashed potato and a green vegetable.

Lady Penn

Presentation of Shamrock to the Micks

One of my happiest memories of Queen Elizabeth concerns Her annual presentation of Shamrock to the Micks and, memorably, the occasion in 1995 when Her Majesty The Queen joined Her in Chelsea for the parade. The Queen had only one concern – that The Queen Mother must not have to climb any stairs. This presented a problem, as one of the most cherished parts of Queen Elizabeth's annual visit was to the Cookhouse, where all the Guardsmen sitting down to lunch thanked Her for Her gift of Shamrock. She then joined the Warrant and Non-Commissioned Officers and their families for a drink in the Sergeants' Mess. Unfortunately the Cookhouse and Sergeants' Mess in Chelsea Barracks were both on an upper floor. However, the Property Services Agency came to the rescue. They declared that the service lift, used to deliver rations to the first floor kitchens, needed to be refurbished, and so it was that as 17 March 1995 approached engineers were beavering away.

The great day dawned, and they were still beavering. By the end of the parade they had finished, but they had not yet tested the new lift. With great trepidation the Commanding Officer escorted both Queens into the lift, and put his hands together in prayer. The doors closed, and The Queen Mother asked why he was praying. 'Because I may be about to be in the most embarrassing position imaginable for a guardsman: stuck in a lift with two Queens, Ma'am'. Queen Elizabeth put Her hands together, followed by The Queen and very slowly the new lift ascended. The parties in the Cookhouse, the Sergeants' Mess and the Officers' Mess were unforgettable, with both Queens on the best form imaginable, even when the Dubonnet in the Sergeants' Mess was found to be off!

Sir Sebastian Roberts

guard of honour

" *In memory of the lamb that we had for lunch in the Irish Guards Officers' Mess almost every year when Queen Elizabeth presented the Shamrock, here is a recipe with the suitable name 'Guard of Honour'. Best end of neck is an economical cut of lamb which looks spectacular if the joints are sewn together, cutlet bones interlaced, like the crossed swords of a guard of honour.* "

SERVES 6-8

2 best end of neck of lamb, each with 8 cutlets
2 oz/50g butter
2 tablespoons olive oil
Sprig of fresh rosemary
2 lb/1kg button onions
2 lb/1kg shelled peas
½ teaspoon caster sugar
Salt and black pepper

Ask your butcher to chine the joints and remove 2 in/5cm of tissue from the top of the bones. Sew the two joints together, skin-side out, so the thick meaty parts form the base and the bones interlace at the top like the swords of a guard of honour. Melt the butter and olive oil in a roasting tin in a preheated oven at 180°C/350°F/Gas 4. Wrap foil round each bone to keep it white while cooking. Place the meat with a sprig of rosemary in the roasting tin, season, then transfer to the centre of the oven and roast for about 90 minutes (allow 25 minutes per lb/450g and 25 minutes extra).

Peel the onions and cook them whole in lightly salted water for 20 minutes, drain and keep hot. Put the peas in a pan with the caster sugar and just enough water to cover them. Bring them to the boil and simmer until just tender. Drain and mix with the onions.

Take the meat from the roasting pan, remove foil and string, and place the guard of honour on a warm dish. Surround it with the vegetables. Serve with redcurrant jelly and lots of murphies.

Sir Sebastian Roberts

Two Tales of Diamond Brooches

Members of the Royal Family are not normally Vice Presidents of anything but The Queen Mother, having been President of the Royal Smithfield Club, joined other past Presidents of the Club and became a Vice President for life. As such She had a badge which declared Her to be a Vice President and She had some concerns about what it was She was 'presiding' over!

At one show She apologised saying that She had forgotten Her badge and, doing my Walter Raleigh bit, I took off my badge and suggested that Her Majesty might wear it. It was accepted and She removed Her large diamond brooch and passed it to me saying, "You can have that". The gleam in my eye must have showed as She followed up with, "For the time being!"

Jim Stobo

Her Majesty Queen Elizabeth The Queen Mother attended a charity auction at Sandown Racecourse one evening in the 1980s. I was involved in finding items for this, including a diamond brooch. There was competitive bidding, as I had asked my husband Jamie to keep up the bidding, because the charity would only be allowed to have the proceeds above a certain price. To my great embarrassment the brooch was finally knocked down to him for a considerable sum. After the auction Queen Elizabeth approached us and said, "We had better not tell Simon (my father-in-law) about this!"

Years later I was wearing the brooch at another event and Queen Elizabeth came up with the warmest of smiles and asked, "Is that THE brooch?" She never forgot an indiscretion!

The Countess of Dalhousie

roast rib of beef

Boned joint rib of beef (at least 5 lbs/2.25kg without bones)
Salt & freshly ground black pepper

4 level tablespoons butter
6-8 tablespoons red wine or stock or water

Preheat oven to 250°C/500°F/Gas 9 and wait 20 minutes to get it properly hot. Rub joint with the salt and pepper and spread on the butter. Place on a rack on a roasting tin. Roast for 3 minutes per lb/450g of beef and then switch off the oven. DO NOT OPEN THE OVEN DOOR. After 2 hours test the meat for heat. If it is still hot it is ready to serve. Otherwise reheat at the same temperature for about 10 minutes. Transfer the joint to a platter and leave for 15 minutes at front of the oven with the door open. Use the juices and sediment that remains reinforced with the wine, stock or water in the tin to make a gravy. The beef will have an outer crust but will be pink inside and juicy.

The Earl of Caithness

Her Majesty Queen Elizabeth The Queen Mother with some of Her Aberdeen Angus

june's pizza
with a cheese scone mixture base

8 oz/225g homemade cheese scone mixture
8 oz/225g back bacon, snipped
1 large onion, chopped finely
1 tin tomatoes with herbs
4 oz/100g grated cheddar cheese
2 oz/50g finely grated Parmesan

Make scone mixture and line a swiss roll tin with it. Fry off bacon and onions and layer on top of scone mixture. Spread over tomatoes and cheese. Bake in centre of oven 180°C/350°F/Gas 4 for 30 to 35 minutes or until the scone mix is cooked. Remove and sprinkle with Parmesan.

Good hot or cold.

June Webster

stuffed cabbage
cabbage made delicious!

1 large cabbage (about 2-3 lb/1.5 kg)
1 red pepper, chopped
½ green pepper, chopped
1 large onion, chopped
1 tin chopped tomatoes

1 teaspoon mixed herbs
2 cloves garlic, chopped
1 lb/450g pork sausage meat
½ pint/300ml stock (can be made with stock cube)
Breadcrumbs

Scoop out centre of cabbage and cook as separate vegetable. Place whole outer cabbage in casserole and fill with the mixed ingredients, (chopped peppers, onion, garlic, tomatoes, herbs and sausage meat). Pour over stock and sprinkle breadcrumbs on top.

Bake with lid on in a moderate oven (180°C/350°F/Gas 4) for approximately 1¼ hours, removing lid for last 15 minutes. Thicken stock, if desired.

Joan Miller

leek and bacon tart with thyme

a really easy quick supper dish

SERVES 4

1 shallot, finely chopped
1 oz/25g butter
1 or 2 trimmed leeks 7oz/175g in total
4 rashers smoked streaky bacon
1 teaspoon fresh thyme or ½ teaspoon dried thyme

2 large organic eggs
2 generous tablespoons soured cream
8 in/20cm ready-made savoury pastry case
   (or homemade if preferred)
3 tablespoons grated Parmesan

Preheat the oven to 200°C/400°F/Gas 6. Melt the butter in a sauté pan and gently fry the shallot. Wash, trim and slice the leeks into ½ in/1cm slices. Chop the bacon and cook alongside the shallot until golden. Add the well drained leeks, salt and pepper. Cover and cook until tender, turning once or twice, for about 15 minutes. Whisk the eggs and sour cream and season again with salt and pepper and the thyme. Spread the leeks in the pastry case. Pour over the custard and scatter grated Parmesan over the top. Bake for 20 minutes or until golden and the topping is puffed up and set.

Felicity Colville

zucchini slice

a starter or light summer dish served with a nice salad

SERVES 6

12 oz/375g zucchini (courgettes)
1 large onion
3 rashers bacon
4 oz/1 cup grated cheddar cheese

4 oz/100g self raising flour
5 floz/120ml oil
5 eggs, beaten
Salt and pepper

Grate unpeeled zucchini coarsely. Finely chop onion and bacon. Combine all ingredients. Pour into dish as for a quiche and bake for 30 to 40 minutes.

A starter or light summer dish served with a nice salad.

Jane Walker-Okeover

73

homemade hamburgers

> *Honestly, there is no comparison between a homemade hamburger and a shop-bought one. Here is a recipe I've used for years and years because everyone enjoys them – and children love making them too, which keeps them quiet on a Saturday morning! The recipe is basically the same as for steak tartare and is ideal for barbecuing as well as frying.*

Allow a generous 4oz/100g ORDINARY mince per person (preferably from a butcher shop). Place the mince in a large bowl and add a good dollop of olive oil, one egg yolk per lb/450g, plenty of Lea and Perrins, some salt, some chopped parsley (scissored up in a mug) and a little crushed garlic.

Plunge your clean hands into this unedifying mess, mix and knead it thoroughly, scoop out a handful and roll it round and round to form a gently squashed disc. Keep going, placing finished hamburgers on a flat plate or tray, and then allow the flavours to be absorbed for a bit (or overnight).

Barbecue or fry over a high heat so that the outside is dark brownish and the inside still pink. Rest before eating. Beware not to overcook them and lose that delicious moist inside. Once removed they still go on cooking without telling you. Place in a warm buttered roll and top with ketchup and rings of raw onion – absolutely wonderful!

Lady Edmonstone

north ronaldsay mutton

" This recipe was created by Philip Corrick, Executive Chef of the Royal Automobile Club, Pall Mall, London, to celebrate the inaugural Mey Selections North Ronaldsay Mutton Run in October 2008. "

SERVES 4

1½ lb/600g small diced leg of mutton
3 oz/80g chopped carrot
3 oz/80g chopped onion
2 oz/50g chopped leek
½ teaspoon plain flour
Tomato purée, to taste
1 pint/500ml brown mutton stock
Salt and pepper
Fresh mint leaves
Cooking oil
2 oz/50g cooked pearl barley

For the hot water pastry
¼ pint/125ml water
4 oz/185g butter
8 oz/250g plain flour
Pinch of salt

For the thyme jus
2 oz/50g chopped shallot
2 oz/50g butter
Sprigs of fresh thyme
1 measure whisky
1 pint/½ litre brown mutton stock

For the pie, seal the seasoned mutton in a very hot pan, add the vegetables, cook gently together, add a little flour, cook out a little. Add a touch of tomato purée, cover with stock and simmer gently or braise covered with a lid in the oven. When cooked, correct the seasoning, cool, then add the pearl barley and a little chopped mint.

For the pastry, place the water, butter and a pinch of salt in a pan and boil. Add the flour, cook until the mixture leaves the sides of the pan, then place in a bowl to cool and refrigerate until required. Roll out and line 3 in/80mm stainless steel rings, place the pie filling in the mould, then cover with a pastry top. Bake at 200°C/400°F/Gas 6 for 12-15 minutes.

To make the jus, place the shallot in a pan with half the butter and the sprigs of thyme. Sweat without colour, flame with the whisky, then add the stock and reduce to a sauce consistency. Whisk in the remaining butter, season and strain the sauce. To serve, place the pie at the top of the plate. Arrange a neat pile of vegetables and pour the sauce around.

Dick Turpin

pork italienne

a family favourite

SERVES 4 (generously!)

1 tablespoon oil
12 trimmed pork fillet medallions, beaten thinly
1 large onion, sliced
1 clove garlic, sliced
4 tomatoes, halved and seeds removed

¾ pint/450ml white wine
6 ozs/150g mushrooms, sliced
¾ pint/450ml double or whipping cream (or a mix
    of cream and crème fraîche)
Salt and pepper, to taste

Heat the oil in a frying pan and add the pork, sealing both sides. Add the onions, mixing them through the pork. Add the tomato halves with the slices of garlic placed inside them. Add white wine and salt and pepper to taste. Cook on a medium to high heat for 10 to 15 minutes until the wine has reduced and by which time the pork should be tender. Add the mushrooms, stirring them through. Add the cream and crème fraîche until it thickens and the mushrooms are cooked. Serve up giving each person 3 pieces of pork fillet and two pieces of tomato each, and a share of the sauce on top.

Barbara Hiddleston

**A North Country Cheviot
sheep in the Dining Room**

baked ham florentina
with nutmeg, carbonara sauce and mustard

SERVES 4
9 oz/240g packet baby spinach
10 oz/280g jar carbonara
   or cheese sauce
4 slices ham (about 7 oz/200g total
   weight), cut from the bone
1 teaspoon ready-prepared
   English mustard
2 pinches ground nutmeg
Black pepper
1 slice stale bread

Put the baby spinach in a large pan with the sauce, nutmeg and mustard and season well with black pepper. Bring to the boil and cook for 2 minutes or until it is wilted and the sauce is bubbling.

Fold ham into quarters and arrange in an ovenproof dish. Spoon creamy spinach mixture over the ham and sprinkle with roughly processed crumbs made from the bread. Bake at 200°C/400°F Gas 6 for 20-25 minutes or until golden and bubbling.

Serve with mixed herbs and salad leaves.

Christina Murray

"I am Your Majesty's Hereditary Carver!"

During the summer of 1987, *HMY Britannia* was being refitted, which that year put paid to the Western Isles Cruise so much enjoyed by Her Majesty The Queen and other members of The Royal Family. By way of recompense Her Majesty Queen Elizabeth The Queen Mother kindly suggested that Her Majesty The Queen might like to come and stay at the Castle of Mey for a few days. This was a novel experience, for although The Queen with Her family had visited the Castle of Mey practically every August since 1956, Her Majesty had never spent a night there.

On leaving the Coldstream Guards in 1959, Major Sir Ralph Anstruther Bt. joined Her Majesty Queen Elizabeth The Queen Mother's Household and was latterly Her Majesty's Treasurer. Sir Ralph was, in fact, a double baronet, and with his title, the 11th Baronet of Anstruther, came also the title of Hereditary Carver to The Sovereign, an honour granted to the family in 1585 by King James VI.

Quite when the Hereditary Carver to the Sovereign was last regularly engaged in the noble art is uncertain, but Sir Ralph's chance came that summer in 1987 and he was not slow to grasp the opportunity. Breakfast at Mey in Her late Majesty's day was a wonderfully civilised affair and there was invariably a large York ham on the sideboard. As Her Majesty The Queen made Her way to the sideboard Sir Ralph sprung to his feet and seizing the ham knife exclaimed, 'Please allow me, Ma'am, for I am Your Majesty's Hereditary Carver!' and proceeded to expertly slice the ham. I suspect that it gave Sir Ralph tremendous pleasure to actually fulfil his inherited role.

Ashe Windham

Tea or a Drink?

In August 1996 I had organised to go and see the McCarthys at Longoe Farm. I was hoping to purchase an Aberdeen Angus heifer to help me start up a small pedigree herd at Binscarth to run alongside my commercial herd of one hundred and fifty AA Simmental-cross cows. Queen Elizabeth heard of this pending visit and invited us to stay.

We arrived at the Castle of Mey at 6pm and were met by Her Majesty, the Lady-in-Waiting and the Equerry Major Charlie MacEwan. After the normal formalities we were asked whether we would like tea or a drink. As it was early evening, I was in rather a quandary whether to opt for tea or a drink, but to be safe I opted for tea. I think this was the wrong decision! Tea for two was served in the drawing room and while Jane and I tucked into cucumber sandwiches and tea, Queen Elizabeth and the others chatted away to us; but you could see there was eager anticipation for us to finish. As soon as we had, Queen Elizabeth immediately said, "Lovely! Shall we all now have a drink?"

The only other guest was Air Commodore Sir Archie Winskill, who had flown Spitfires during the Second World War and had been Captain of the Queen's Flight for many years. Sir Archie sat on Her Majesty's right and I had the honour of sitting on Her left. Queen Elizabeth was an expert at making you feel relaxed. She was very attentive and would speak to you for a whole course and then speak to the other guest during the next course. After dinner we retired to the library and sat down to watch a *Dad's Army* video that Sir Archie had brought as a present.

The following day Her Majesty showed us around Her walled garden and we visited Her AA pedigree herd at Longoe. I remember this visit to the Castle of Mey more vividly than the times She came to Grindelay for lunch and it will always bring back fond memories of Her Majesty Queen Elizabeth The Queen Mother.

Malcolm Macrae

Her Majesty Queen Elizabeth The Queen Mother and the brothers Danny and Sandy McCarthy in 1990 with a prize-winning Aberdeen Angus bull and North Country Cheviot sheep

poultry & game

A useful chicken in the Castle of Mey Kitchen

The Lonely Grouse

12th August 2000

They shot only one grouse today, 'The Glorious Twelfth'. We put it on an enormous salva with a cover and presented it to the expectant diners, with as much ceremonial pomp as we could muster (in the few steps from the pantry to the dining room) with much mirth from the diners. Captain William de Rouet carved the little bird into nine pieces (there must have been nine dining) as Queen Elizabeth instructed, using the same graceful swordsmanship he showed on Her Majesty's 100th birthday when he opened Her telegram from The Queen. If one of us had picked up a sword to do that, we would have probably sliced someone's arm off. Incidentally no one went hungry as there was also lamb.

Entry from the diary of Bruce Guest

game crumble

1 small jar of tomato pesto
   (tomato and almond pesto works well too)
Approximately 4 game birds
   (Pheasants, partridges etc – judge the meat
   content by allowing one or two breasts of meat
   per person and the leg meat for the pot)
2 or 3 onions, roughly chopped
2 carrots, roughly chopped
2 or 3 bay leaves
A few sticks of celery, chopped
1 leek, chopped

Juniper berries
Light chicken stock or water
Butter

For the crumble
8 oz (225g) plain flour
3 oz (75g) butter
or
8 oz (225g) breadcrumbs
Some butter
Some grated Parmesan cheese

Casserole the meat by placing it in a roomy cooking pot and cover with water or light chicken stock. Add the roughly chopped carrots, onions, some sticks of celery and a leek if you have it. Throw in a few juniper berries, a pinch of salt and ground black pepper and the bay leaves. Bring to a gentle simmer but do not boil. Remove any scum that rises to the surface. Cook like this for 20 minutes. Turn off the heat and leave to settle. When cool enough, remove all the bones taking care to detect any small sharp ones. Boil up the remaining liquid and reduce greatly to concentrate the flavour.

Make the crumble by rubbing the butter and flour together thoroughly in a bowl or whizz in an electric blender. (For a breadcrumb topping whizz some slightly stale crustless bread in a blender and sprinkle this over the meat mixture. Dot with butter and sprinkle with some grated Parmesan cheese.) Coat the cooked meat with some of the reduced stock and all the pesto. Pile it into an ovenproof serving dish. Sprinkle over the crumble mix and dot with butter. Place in a pre-heated oven at 180°C/350°F/Gas 4 for 30 to 40 minutes.

This is a lunch, dinner or supper dish. Perhaps serve it with a salad and some plainly cooked potatoes at lunch; a selection of vegetables at dinner. For supper it just needs some good bread. You can use game birds or just chicken and of course it works wonders with leftover turkey at Christmas. It can be frozen only if the meat hasn't been previously frozen. To make more of a sauce you need to add a little more stock in proportion to the pesto, but if in doubt make more sauce so that the crumble won't dry out if it needs to be kept warm for longer. (Royalty are very good at timekeeping at meal times but you never know who has been invited for dinner who might hold things up.)

Bruce Guest

"Have you got a bird?"

I had only been an equerry for about three weeks and was still rather green to the new role. It was at Clarence House, while at lunch one day, that I got a sense of the 'character' I was going to be working for. There were only three of us for lunch that day, The Queen Mother, the Lady-in-Waiting and myself. I was enjoying my starter when Her Majesty asked me if I had a girlfriend or, as She understood was the more modern parlance, did I have a 'bird'? Somewhat taken back at the terminology, I replied, "At the moment I have neither. But 'bird'?! That is very with it!" Her Majesty thought about it for a moment and replied, "Well William, I am very with it!" I always used that as the benchmark for the type of person She was: ninety-eight years old, former Queen of England, but still very 'with it'.

William de Rouet

pheasant bake

1 pheasant (you can use just pheasant breasts
   if that's all you have taken off the bird)
2 oz/50g butter
2 large onions
1 clove garlic, finely chopped
½ pint/300ml water

4 oz/100g streaky bacon
3 oz/75g breadcrumbs
2 teaspoons flour
1 beaten egg
3 tablespoons cream
1 tablespoon grainy mustard

Poach the pheasant with half the butter and half an onion and the garlic in a pan. Cover with the water and cook slowly for 1 to 1½ hours (30 to 45 minutes if using just pheasant breasts). Meanwhile, fry the bacon until crisp and then add the breadcrumbs and combine to make a crispy topping. Once the pheasant is cooked, shred the meat and put into an ovenproof dish (I find using two forks to shred the meat works quite well). Retain the stock. For the sauce, chop the remaining onion and cook in the remaining butter. Once the butter is soft, stir in the flour. Strain the stock that the pheasant was poached in and add slowly to the onions and flour, stirring continuously to avoid lumps. Add up to 1 pint/600ml of the liquid, the more sauce the better. Cook for 5 minutes and then slowly add the beaten egg, cream and mustard. Pour over the pheasant and then spread the bacon and breadcrumb topping over. Heat in a preheated oven at 180°C/350°F/Gas 4 until crispy. If intending to put straight in the freezer, cook the pheasant and the sauce and combine in the ovenproof dish and then freeze. When ready to use, defrost the mixture, then add the topping before it goes in the oven.

William de Rouet

congham pigeon breasts in red wine

SERVES 4
8 pigeon breasts
Olive oil
Red wine
Butter for frying
Chopped onion
Stock
Bay leaf

Beforehand, marinate the pigeon in olive oil and red wine for a few hours. Panfry the pigeon breasts in butter until cooked but still pink in the middle – keep warm. Use the same pan for frying the chopped onion. Add red wine and reduce by half. Add the stock, some ground pepper and a bay leaf and reduce to taste. Pour over the pigeon breasts and serve.

Henry Bellingham
Henry Bellingham lives in Congham, Norfolk, hence the name for his recipe

venischnitzel

Slices of venison from the haunch (or fillet), ¼-½ in thick
Flour
Beaten egg
Breadcrumbs

Beat the venison slices with a meat tenderiser or put them between sheets of cling film and beat them with a rolling pin so that they are really thin. Dip them in flour, then beaten egg and then breadcrumbs and fry in oil until lightly brown and serve with redcurrant or rowan jelly and perhaps a wedge of lemon or some fried fresh parsley.

You can prepare them in advance up to the frying stage but once they have been fried they should be served immediately. I do not always include the flour stage but a classic Wiener Schnitzel, from which the idea comes, does include the flour.

Catriona Leslie

honey curried chicken
deliciously coated chicken

4 chicken breasts with skins on
2 oz/50g butter
4 oz/100g clear honey
2 oz/50g Dijon mustard
1 tablespoon curry powder
Salt and pepper

Preheat the oven to 190°C/375°F/Gas 5. Melt the butter and add the curry powder. Stir in the honey and mustard and season to taste. Place chicken in a greased ovenproof dish and coat in the honey mix. Roast for 30 minutes, turning the chicken halfway through the cooking time and making sure that the chicken is cooked through.

Ann Baird

cheat's chicken pie

1 large onion, diced
2 sticks celery, chopped
2 carrots, diced
8 chicken thighs (boned and skinned) and
      cut into bite-size chunks

1 or 2 small tins condensed chicken soup
Salt and pepper to taste
Milk (if required)
Puff pastry
Egg wash

Boil the celery and carrots for approx 10 minutes to ensure fully cooked when in the pie. Drain well. Fry them off with the onion in a spoonful of oil and a knob of butter. Tip into a large pie dish. Fry off the chicken chunks and add to the pie dish. Pour in the chicken soup – as much as is necessary. This is the cheat as it now becomes the sauce in the pie! If more sauce is required, then swill out the tins with the milk – do not use water. Season to taste.

Top with the puff pastry and brush with a little egg wash. Bake at 180°C/350°F/Gas 4 for approximately 30 minutes until the pastry is golden and well cooked. Serve with creamy mashed potatoes and green vegetables.

Susan Murray

brazilian chicken rio
exotic cooking in Mey!

SERVES 4
3 oranges
4 chicken portions (breast is best)
Salt
½ level teaspoon paprika
2 oz/50g butter
2 level tablespoons plain flour
½ level tablespoon brown sugar
¼ level teaspoon ground ginger

Pare rind of 1 orange and cut rind into strips. Squeeze juice from rinded orange and also from the second. Add some water to juice to make up ½ pint/300ml.

Divide each chicken portion into 4 strips and sprinkle with salt and paprika. Melt butter in a deep frying pan and add chicken and brown off. Remove chicken pieces. Stir flour into dripping in pan together with sugar and ginger. Stir in juice and rind. Bring to the boil and boil for 2 to 3 minutes. Check seasoning. Put everything into a casserole and cook in a moderate oven (180°C/350°F/Gas 4) for 40 to 45 minutes or until chicken is tender. Peel third orange and divide into segments free of membrane. Add to casserole during last few minutes of cooking time.

Serve with rice to which parsley has been added.

June Webster

chicken tropicana

“ *This dish was inspired by the famous Coco Mania given to Queen Elizabeth by Noël Coward when in 1965 She visited him in his Jamaican home.* ”

SERVES 4

4 lb/2kg large chicken
4 coconuts (1 whole coconut per guest; adjust other ingredients if more used)
2 red peppers
2 green peppers
2 onions

6 oz/175g fresh corn off the cob (or 1 tin sweet corn)
4 oz/100g mushrooms
Cornflour
Salt and pepper to taste
2 tablespoons plain flour mixed to a thick paste with cold water

Wash and dry the coconuts. Punch through the three indentations at the top of each coconut and drain liquid through a fine sieve into a container. Carefully saw off the top of each coconut to make a lid. Put the coconut shells to one side for later use. Place the chicken and coconut milk in a large saucepan with a tightly fitting lid. Gently simmer the chicken until almost tender. Remove the chicken and skin and bone it. Cut chicken meat into small pieces and replace in the saucepan with the liquid. Add chopped peppers, chopped mushrooms, chopped onion, corn and seasoning to taste. Simmer until peppers are soft, adding a little water if necessary. The sauce when cooking should be a little thicker than milk so if necessary add a little mixed cornflour to bring to this consistency. When cooked fill the coconuts.

Using the flour and water paste, very carefully seal the lids on to the bases and also ensure the top holes are re-sealed. This is most important as if this is not done properly the contents will dry out. Put the coconuts into the oven (150°C/300°F/Gas mark 3/Aga roasting oven) for 1½ hours to heat the shells and contents thoroughly. After removing from the oven the coconuts will now retain their heat for 2-3 hours. Serve each coconut unopened on a soup plate with a knife and spoon. A folded napkin can provide a suitable base.

Note: The coconut flesh acts as an insulator and it is not intended for consumption. Over enthusiastic guests have, on occasion, had to be restrained to prevent damage to the dining room table! This is good for lunches, dinner parties, or even picnics and I have used it for twelve guests on occasions. As the coconuts retain their heat there is a rather baffling lack of concern about anything happening in the kitchen! I do need help though with sawing the coconut tops off to make the lids!

Helen Ball

Chicken Tropicana as cooked by Helen Ball

coronation chicken
an old favourite

2 lb/1kg cooked chicken, ¾ in/2cm diced
3 sticks celery, ¾ in/2cm diced
6 tablespoons good mayonnaise (soured cream and/or crème fraîche can be used as an alternative)
2 tablespoons madras curry paste
2 tablespoons mango chutney
8 drops Tabasco sauce or a small pinch of cayenne pepper

Mix the chicken and celery pieces together in a large bowl. In a separate bowl mix together the mayonnaise, curry paste, chutney and Tabasco, ensuring the mixture is thoroughly blended. Add the sauce to the chicken pieces and mix well.

This dish can be served immediately or refrigerated and covered overnight to allow the flavours to meld and mature. It has traditionally been served with a rice salad and plain lettuce.

Michael Sealey

easy supper dish
prepare in the morning to cook later

SERVES 2 or 4 (depending on how hungry you are!)

4 chicken thighs
6 spring onions
6 cherry tomatoes
6 sliced mushrooms
¼ pint/150ml stock
¼ pint/150ml wine or vermouth

Brown the chicken on both sides in a little olive oil and place in an ovenproof dish. Add the sliced spring onions, tomatoes quartered and the sliced mushrooms. Season well, then add the stock and the wine or vermouth. Bake in a preheated oven at 180°C/350°F/Gas 4 for approximately 40 minutes until cooked.

Can be prepared in the morning to cook later.

Jenny Gordon-Lennox

caithness chicken casserole

" Dad liked this made with pork instead of chicken. "

2 chicken fillets, skinned
4 oz/100g smoked bacon, chopped
15ml cooking oil
1 oz/25g butter
1 onion, cut into rings
1 stalk celery, diced
2 oz/50g mushrooms
Pinch of freshly chopped or dried thyme

½ teaspoon basil
1 teaspoon garlic paste
Salt and ground black pepper
2½ floz/75ml cider
2½ floz/75ml chicken stock
2 tablespoons double cream
Parsley for garnish
1 teaspoon cornflour blended with a little water

Pre-heat oven to temperature 190°C/375°F/Gas 5. Heat oil and fry chicken lightly with the garlic paste. Place in a casserole. Fry chopped bacon lightly. Add butter to pan and fry onion and celery. Fry sliced mushrooms. Add herbs, seasoning, stock and cider to pan and boil up. Pour over chicken. Cover and bake for 1 hour.

Arrange chicken on heated serving dish and keep hot. Add blended cornflour to casserole and cook 2 to 3 minutes to thicken. Add the cream and pour sauce over chicken. Garnish and serve with a green salad and baked potato.

Wilma Stewart
*Wilma Stewart won 1st prize in the Highland Region
for Junior Cook of the Year in 1985, aged 12 years*

venison olives
serve with creamed potatoes and parsley garnish

Each October on Her journey from Birkhall to the Castle of Mey, The Queen Mother would call for lunch at Glenmazeran, the Highland estate of Her nephew, Lord Elphinstone. Gladys Davidson was Lord Elphinstone's cook, and Duncan Davidson and Ian (my husband) were keepers on the estate. Gladys created her delicious recipes from game, fish, fruit and vegetables from the estate. Her Majesty enjoyed Her venison olives very much. This is my version of the recipe, but I'm sure that Gladys had some extra magic ingredients to add!

SERVES 4

8 thin slices of uncooked haunch venison
1 carrot
1 small turnip
1 celery stalk
1 onion
1 tablespoon chopped parsley
3 oz/75g fresh breadcrumbs

Bouquet garni
¾ pint/450ml beef stock
2 oz/50g butter
1 oz/25g flour, seasoned
1 oz/25g suet
1 egg
Creamed potato

Cut the vegetables into small pieces and fry lightly in the butter. Remove from pan. Mix the suet, parsley, breadcrumbs, and seasoning with the egg. Spread on the venison slices and roll up. Tie with string, roll each olive in seasoned flour and brown in a pan.

Place the olives in a casserole with the vegetables, cover with the stock and add the bouquet garni. Simmer for 1½ to 2 hours. Remove the string and bouquet garni. Place in warm serving dish. Pipe creamed potato around the edge and garnish with parsley.

(Recipe photographed on page 97)

Betty Watson

Opposite: The purple Scottish heather
Opposite (inset): Her Majesty Queen Elizabeth The Queen Mother with Ian and Betty Watson at Glenmazeran

"After lunch, The Queen Mother often liked to walk out a little way to listen to the stags roaring in the hills. She was always interested in the work on the estate and invariably asked if it had been a good year for fishing in the nearby River Findhorn. She loved the gentians and heather which grew around the Lodge, and on Her departure I would give Her a little posy to take with Her on Her journey to Mey. She used to break off a sprig of the heather and tuck it into Her hat. I feel very privileged to have met Her: She was a truly gracious lady."

grouse in aspic

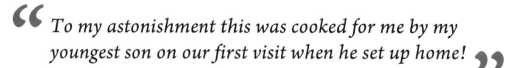

My mother-in-law, Bett Murray, spent some of her childhood at Balmoral where her father, Lieutenant Colonel Alec Mackenzie, was the last King's Commissioner. He was sacked by King Edward VIII and not replaced. Bett always said she disliked cooking immensely but the marvellous lunches and dinners she plied us with over the years were legion and totally delicious. This recipe is one of them, which she valiantly made even though she never liked eating grouse herself.

Braise the grouse with some good stock, onions, parsley, bay leaf and some sherry. When cooked carve the breasts. Mince a little ham with the meat from the legs and some cream. Meat pate is a good substitute for the leg meat if time is scarce. Place the meat 'mousse' in bottom of a dish. Lay the sliced grouse breasts and some small cooked carrots cut into rounds on top in a pattern. Sprinkle with some chopped fresh parsley. Cover with aspic jelly made with stock from the grouse. Serve with salad and new potatoes.

Christina Murray

duck a la nicholas

To my astonishment this was cooked for me by my youngest son on our first visit when he set up home!

SERVES 2

2 duck breasts	2 teaspoons lemon juice
1 orange, zested and juiced	20 floz/480ml of water
1 tablespoon sugar	1 chicken stock cube
1 tablespoon white vinegar	2 tablespoons Grand Marnier or Cointreau

Quickly brown the duck breasts on both sides. Put sauce ingredients into saucepan and boil until reduced by half, then add 1 tablespoon of cornflour slaked with water. Add the Grand Marnier or Cointreau. Cook the duck in a preheated oven at 200°C/400°F/Gas 6 for 20 minutes. Slice and serve with sauce. Orange segments can be used as decoration.

Sheila Farley-Sutton

Venison Olives cooked by Lance Purcell
(see recipe on page 94)

pheasant in mango chutney

" This is an old favourite of mine and will convert even those who proclaim not to like game into addicts! It was a great standby during my bachelor days when the supply of pheasants seemed inexhaustible and the time to deal with them was limited as the working day was a long one! Most of the work for this recipe can be done the previous evening. I am sometimes reminded, when preparing this dish, of Mr Michael Sealey, who was Her late Majesty's Head Chef for many years. He had an aversion, bordering on horror, of game in the feather and was only slightly more pleased to see fish with their heads on! Many was the time that we approached the kitchen windows at Mey after a successful shooting expedition with a few grouse and a request from Her Majesty that they were to be prepared for dinner that evening. This was usually sufficient to send Michael to the furthest regions of the kitchen and one of his assistants invariably had to handle them for him! "

Place two whole plucked and dressed pheasants into a 200°C/400°F/Gas 6 oven for 30 minutes. Take out the pheasants and let them cool down. Once cool, cut all the slightly underdone meat off the pheasants, extracting the sinews from the leg meat, and place in large ovenproof dish with any juices, though discarding the fat and skin.

Stir a jar 12oz/360g of mango chutney into the pheasant meat and leave to marinate for a few hours or even better overnight. Whip ¾ pint/450ml of double cream until just stiff and spoon over the top of the pheasant dish and sprinkle some paprika pepper on top.

Place the dish into a preheated 220°C/425°F/Gas 7 oven for 20 minutes and then serve with a mixture of basmati and wild rice and mange tout.

Opposite: Chef's nightmare – a guest's gift of game birds in the kitchen at Mey   **Ashe Windham**

chicken in a chive and tarragon herb crust

" I find this freezes very well and only takes a few hours to thaw before cooking. "

SERVES 4

4 chicken breasts, boned and skinned
2 tablespoons freshly chopped tarragon
2 tablespoons freshly chopped chives
1½ oz/45g finely grated parmesan cheese
Salt and freshly ground black pepper

1½ oz/45g butter softened
1-2 cloves garlic, crushed
1-2 tablespoons extra virgin olive oil
1½ oz/45g fresh white breadcrumbs

Put the butter in a mixing bowl and beat well. Add the herbs, garlic, oil, cheese and breadcrumbs and mix thoroughly (I mix it in the food processor). Season with salt and pepper. Spread this paste over the chicken breasts and chill for 15 minutes (or longer). Place the breasts on a baking sheet and bake for 25 minutes at 180°C/375°F/Gas 5.

You can use any other soft herbs such as parsley and dill.

Catriona Leslie

pulled and grilled chicken

SERVES 4
3 lb/1.5kg chicken
1 carrot, cut in half
1 onion, quartered
1 bay leaf
1 stick celery, cut in half
1 sprig of fresh rosemary

For the sauce
1½ oz/37g butter
1½ oz/37g plain flour
¼ pint/150ml single or double cream
Salt and pepper

For the grill coating
2 oz/50g butter
1½ oz/37g plain flour
1 egg yolk
¾ oz/20g tomato purée
Salt and pepper
3 drops Tabasco sauce
3 drops Worcestershire sauce
½ teaspoon French mustard
¾ oz/20g mango chutney
3 oz/75g fresh white breadcrumbs

Place the chicken, vegetables and herbs in a very large saucepan and cover completely with water. Cover and bring to the boil slowly. Reduce the heat and simmer for at least an hour or until the chicken is fully cooked and the juices run clear. Remove the chicken and set aside. Strain the stock and allow it to cool. For the sauce, melt the butter in a medium-sized saucepan. Once melted add the flour, then stir and allow it to cook for 1 minute. Add the reserved stock gradually, whisking continuously until the sauce thickens and comes to the boil. Allow to simmer for 5 minutes, again whisking continuously to avoid sticking or lumps forming. Once the sauce has cooled, slightly add the cream and season with salt and pepper to taste.

Skin the chicken, then chop the white flesh into bite-sized pieces and add to the sauce, place in a serving bowl, cover and keep warm until serving. Remove the dark meat, cut into bite-sized pieces and set aside. For the grill coating, cream together the butter and flour. Add the remaining ingredients, except the breadcrumbs, and blend until smooth. Coat the dark meat pieces in the mixture and then roll the coated meat in the breadcrumbs and place on a grill pan. Grill the pieces until heated through and golden brown. To serve, place the grilled pieces in a serving bowl and serve separately but alongside the chicken-in-sauce mixture.

This dish was traditionally served with mashed potatoes and green vegetables. At Christmas time, especially on Boxing Day, it was made with leftover turkey and during the shooting season it was made with pheasant.

Michael Sealey

kate's 'meal in a pot'

SERVES 4

1½ lb/1.25kg trimmed leeks
10 oz/275g potatoes
1 tablespoon oil
2 large cloves garlic
7 oz/175g cream cheese

4 floz/100ml white wine
6 floz/175ml chicken stock
2 rounded tablespoon cornflour
8 skinless and boneless chicken thighs
Herbs to flavour
Salt and pepper

Wash and thickly slice the leeks. Peel the potatoes and slice very thinly. Heat the oil in a flame-proof casserole. Add crushed garlic and leeks and cook for about 5 minutes or until beginning to soften. Meanwhile place the cheese, wine, stock and cornflour in a food processor and blend for about 30 seconds or until smooth.

Arrange chicken thighs on top of the leek mixture, pour the cheese mixture over and season to taste. Layer the potatoes over the chicken. Place a lightly oiled sheet of greaseproof paper over the potatoes and then cover the casserole with a lid or foil.

Cook in a preheated oven at 180°C/350°F/Gas 4 for 1½ hours or until the potatoes are quite tender. Brown the potatoes under the grill.

This dish can be prepared the day before, and then reheated and browned under the grill.

Sue Jenkins

chicken in a champagne sauce

" This is a very easy and elegant dish to prepare and your guests will be very impressed with your cooking ability when you present it to them. I have had many requests for this recipe over the years and have happily shared it with so many friends. I hope you will enjoy it as well. "

SERVES 2
1 whole chicken breast, halved and skinned
2 tablespoons of butter, divided
2 tablespoons chopped shallots
6 floz/170ml champagne
2½ floz/60ml double cream
Pinch of salt

Place the chicken breast halves between sheets of waxed paper or cling film and pound lightly until about ½ in/1.25cm thick. Heat half of the butter in a skillet over a medium high heat. Add the chicken and cook for about 3 minutes on each side or until golden brown and cooked through. Remove to a plate and keep warm.

Add the shallots to the skillet and cook gently until translucent. Pour in the Champagne and cook over a high heat until reduced by half. Add the cream and salt, cooking until the sauce thickens slightly. Whisk in the remaining tablespoon of butter. Arrange the chicken on 2 plates and top with the sauce. Serve with rice or potatoes and seasonal vegetables. Enjoy!

Above: a real flower ice bucket created by Bruce Guest

Judith Maddocks

A tantalus in the
Dining Room at Mey

The Last Captain of the Queen's Flight

Air Commodore The Hon. Sir Timothy Elworthy KCVO CBE was the last of a very distinguished line of Captains of The Queen's Flight, and like the first holder of the post, Sir Edward Fielden, was a firm favourite of Her late Majesty's. I can well remember one of Tim's final visits to the Castle of Mey when he was overseeing the arrangements to fly Her Majesty from Wick to Aberdeen at the end of Queen Elizabeth's four-week August holiday in Caithness. Her Majesty had asked him to lunch and I recall taking him up the tower to look at the views across the Pentland Firth and into the walled garden on a wonderful bright late summer forenoon. On descending he had steadfastly refused all offers of alcoholic refreshment, proffered by sundry equerries, but once seated next to Her Majesty at luncheon he was powerless to refuse Her offer of a glass of wine. "There is no use putting your hand over your glass, Tim, for William (Tallon) will simply pour it through your fingers," Her Majesty remarked! Discretion forbids me disclosing whether he actually drank any wine whilst on duty that day!

Ashe Windham

thai chicken

SERVES 15-20

2 large chickens, cooked and flesh removed
¼ pint/150ml good olive oil
Juice and zest of 3 limes
2 tablespoons fish sauce
2 cloves crushed garlic

1 medium-sized red chilli, deseeded and chopped
2 stems lemongrass, finely chopped
1 large bunch fresh coriander, finely chopped
Salt and pepper

Mix the above (except the chicken) as a vinaigrette. Add the chicken (preferably warm) cut into bite-sized pieces. Cover and leave in fridge overnight to infuse flavours. It will keep for at least 3 days. Serve it with couscous made with herbs, pine nuts and raisins or whatever you think would go deliciously with it.

Lady Elworthy

The Wild Geese

Every October Her Majesty Queen Elizabeth The Queen Mother would return to the Castle of Mey for Her second visit of the year.

One day whilst going about my duties in the Castle, I met Her Majesty who asked me if I had seen any wild geese arrive for the winter. She then added, "I have seen them every year for fifty years at Mey and I do hope that I see them this year!"
I thought for a minute, then replied, "Sorry Ma'am but I haven't seen any yet, but you still have plenty time to see them before you go."

A few days later I again met Her Majesty, and as She passed me, She whispered, "Still no sign of the geese?" I replied, "No, sorry Ma'am."

Soon the day arrived for The Queen Mother to leave the Castle. That morning She hesitantly came down the front hall stairs and said Her goodbyes to all the staff.

Her Majesty's car drew up outside the front door and just as She was about to step in, to my amazement, a flock of wild geese appeared in the distance. As they flew over the Castle in their V-shaped formation, Her Majesty looked to the sky and Her face lit up. She then turned to us and said, "I'm happy now!"

I knew what She meant. The geese that She had looked for every day had suddenly appeared as if to say goodbye to Her Majesty. Sadly, October 2001 was The Queen Mother's last visit to the Castle of Mey.

Nancy McCarthy

fish & seafood

£ kilos

£

Catch Zone

Scottish

Scotland's larder: the day's catch at market

fish pie

serve with creamed potatoes or on a bed of rice

SERVES 4

1lb/450g mixed smoked and plain haddock,
  cut into small chunks
1½ oz/40g flour
2 oz/50g butter
¾ pint/425ml milk

6 oz/175g grated cheddar cheese
½ teaspoon mustard powder
Salt and pepper
1 onion, finely chopped
4 oz/100g cooked prawns

Dip fish in a little flour and lay half in an ovenproof dish. Melt butter, stir in remaining flour, gradually stir in milk and cook slowly until thickened. Add mustard powder and 4oz/100g of the cheese, and season. Stir until cheese has melted, then add onions and prawns. Pour half of the sauce over the fish in the dish. Place remainder of the fish on top and cover with rest of the sauce. Sprinkle remaining cheese on top. Cook in a preheated oven at 160°C/325°F/Gas 3 for 40 minutes.

Etta Macleod

halibut in orange juice

SERVES 4

4 Halibut steaks
1½ pints/900ml fish stock (stock cube will do)
1 small onion, finely chopped.
½ oz/13g butter
2 teaspoons corn or sunflower oil
6 floz/160ml concentrated orange juice
2 teaspoons chopped fresh tarragon

2 teaspoons chopped parsley
Salt and pepper
2 teaspoons cornflour
1 tablespoon water
¼ pint/150ml soured cream
8 orange segments

Poach the fish for 10 minutes in the fish stock. Remove the fish and remove the skin and bones. Strain the stock liquid and retain ¼ pint/150ml. Fry onion gently in butter and oil, add orange juice, stock, herbs, salt and pepper. Simmer for 3 minutes. Mix cornflour with water and stir into sauce, continuing to stir until boiling. Remove from the heat and stir in cream, then pour over fish and garnish with orange segments.

Sheila Farley-Sutton

roasted mediterranean tuna

a speedy and delicious one-pot meal

SERVES 4
12 oz/350g new potatoes
1 lb/450g fresh tuna
12 oz/350g tin tomatoes
2 dessertspoons capers
2 oz/50g pitted black olives with anchovies
Salt and ground black pepper
A dusting of Parmesan cheese
2 level tablespoons chopped fresh basil,
    plus sprigs to garnish

Cook the scrubbed new potatoes in a large pan of boiling salted water for 20 minutes or until tender. Drain, cut into halves and set aside.

Cut tuna into chunks. Mix together the tomatoes, capers, olives and anchovies and warm for a few minutes. Transfer the mixture to an ovenproof dish, add the halved potatoes and arrange the fish on top. Season with salt and pepper and sprinkle with the Parmesan cheese. Cook at 200°C/400°F/Gas 6 for 10 to 15 minutes or until the fish is cooked.

Sprinkle with the chopped basil and then garnish with basil sprigs before serving.

Emma Bartlett

baked trout

Caithness is blessed with some of the best wild brown trout fishing in these Isles, and lochs such as Watten, St John's and Heilen are legendary for the quality of their trout. One of my favourite pastimes is to have a day at a hill loch trout fishing in the Highlands, preferably with a walk of an hour or two to reach your destination, for you can be fairly sure that only a handful of fishers will have made the effort in the past few months.

Into a rucksack, aside from your fishing tackle, you should pack the following – a box of matches wrapped up in a plastic bag, an old newspaper, a few sticks of kindling, a well seasoned log split into a dozen or so pieces, a can of beer, a length of thick silver foil, a lemon, a twist of foil with a mix of salt and pepper, an ounce or two of butter and a sharp knife.

On arriving at the loch select a sandy beach out of the wind and submerge your can of beer in the loch and get your fishing tackle ready. After an hour or two you will have caught quite enough trout for your companions and yourself.

Build up a small enclosure using stones and light the fire, utilising your materials and old heather stalks and any dead wood in the vicinity. Whilst the fire is burning down nicely, gut the trout and take their heads and tails off before putting them into silver foil with a knob of butter, a squeeze of lemon, and a sprinkling of salt and pepper. Once the fire has burnt down to a nice bed of red embers place the trout wrapped in parcels of silver foil on top of the embers. Turn them after 3 to 4 minutes, and after another 3 to 4 minutes extract them from the embers and they will be beautifully cooked.

You can either eat them with your fingers or if you are really civilised you will have brought an old plate and a knife and fork! I can attest to the fact that children who have heretofore disdainfully regarded their father's offerings of fish in the comfort of their own homes will devour these al fresco offerings with gusto!

Ashe Windham

The catch!

The River Dee (pictured at Braemar) offers some of the finest fishing in Scotland. The three Balmoral 'beats' are located on the south bank, stretching from The Brig O' Dee (near Braemar) down to Dalliefour (near Ballater).

balmoral salmon

" At Balmoral all the Royal Family would lead an outdoor life, but of the ladies, it was The Queen Mother who was the most energetic. Her great passion was for salmon fishing, and this She did with intense concentration for hours on end. She would put on Her waders and old clothes and attempt to catch the biggest salmon She could find. She liked no interruption and took with Her only the simplest of cold picnics. "

SERVES 12
1 8 lb/4kg salmon
2 carrots, sliced
2 small onions, sliced
20 white peppercorns
2 teaspoons of salt
1 dessertspoon of vinegar
Chopped fresh parsley

For the sauce
1 pint/600ml double cream
1½ pints/900ml mayonnaise
1 teaspoon mustard
2 pinches of sugar
Juice of 1 lemon

Rinse salmon, drain and place in a large saucepan or fish kettle with the sliced carrot, onion peppercorns, salt and vinegar. Add water to cover and bring to the boil. Reduce heat and simmer for 5 minutes. Remove from heat and leave salmon to get cold in its liquid. Before serving, slice fish in half, remove skin and bone without breaking up the flesh, and drain well.

For the sauce, whip cream, stir in mayonnaise, and then gradually add mustard, sugar and lemon juice. Serve the cold salmon garnished with the chopped parsley and accompanied by small boiled potatoes and cucumber salad.

Taken from To Set Before a Queen: The Royal Cookery of Mrs McKee *(Gracewing Publishing).*

Mrs Alma McKee was the Chef at Clarence House for Her Majesty The Queen from 1949 until her Accession, and then for Her Majesty Queen Elizabeth The Queen Mother until she retired in 1960.

scottish langoustines with samphire

" Creel-caught Orkney langoustines are perfection. Try them with steamed samphire to make them totally memorable. "

SERVES 2

10 fresh langoustines
Butter and olive oil
2 cloves garlic, chopped
Half a lemon

Salt and white pepper
White wine
2 handfuls samphire (you can buy samphire from the fishmonger already prepared for cooking)

Steam samphire for 5 minutes. When cooked, squeeze over the lemon, add some butter and white pepper and keep warm in a dish, if possible for no longer than 5 minutes. Heat olive oil and some more butter to cover bottom of frying pan and add garlic. Push garlic around pan until it is cooked, then add the langoustines. When the langoustine have turned pink, after about 3 minutes, give them a squeeze of lemon and salt and pepper to taste. Remove from the heat and put on top of the samphire in dish. Quickly deglaze pan with a little white wine and pour juice over the langoustine and samphire. Serve with good mayonnaise, crusty brown bread and extra lemon.

Emma Bartlett

salmon tray bake
delicious and so simple

SERVES 4

4 tablespoons olive oil, plus a bit more for oiling
8 medium potatoes
Salt and pepper
2 teaspoons of dried mixed herbs
4 large salmon fillets

20 asparagus spears or green beans
20 cherry tomatoes, halved
8 slices of parma ham or chorizo or salami
Juice of 1 lemon

Preheat oven to 190°C/375°F/Gas 5. Line a baking tray with baking parchment. Rub with some oil. Thinly slice potatoes with their skins left on. Arrange over tray, without overlapping too much. Season generously, adding mixed herbs and 2 tablespoons of oil. Put in a hot oven for 15 minutes. Remove baking tray from oven, and increase temperature to 220°C/425°F/Gas 7. Lay salmon fillets on potatoes, scattering around asparagus and tomatoes. Put parma ham/chorizo/salami on top, drizzle over rest of oil, put tray back in oven for 10-15mins until cooked through. Squeeze over lemon juice and serve.

Alice Murray

herb crusted salmon

SERVES 2

2 salmon fillets
2 teaspoons Dijon mustard
1 medium onion finely chopped

1 good handful chopped fresh parsley
1 good handful chopped fresh mint
A glug of olive oil

Mix all ingredients except the salmon together and then roll the salmon in the mixture. Put salmon in a frying pan, cooking it for 2 minutes each side. Transfer salmon to preheated hot oven (190°C/375°F/Gas 5) and cook for another 10 minutes. Serve with green vegetables or salad and new potatoes.

Clare Steen

poached fish in lemon cream sauce

" A delicious recipe suitable for any firm white fish or salmon, from a gem of a restaurant in John O' Groats. "

SERVES 4

4 fillets of either cod, haddock, plaice,
   sole or salmon
4 oz/100g butter

10 floz/300ml double cream
5 or 6 slices of lemon, plus extra to garnish
Salt and white pepper

In a pan large enough to take the fillets side by side, add enough water to come about halfway up the fish and two or three slices of lemon. Bring it to the boil and turn the heat right down. Add the fish, skin-side down, and poach for about 5 minutes, turning once halfway through. Test the fish is cooked by pushing a needle or thin bladed knife through the thickest part of the fillet; there should be no resistance. When cooked, drain off the water and add the remaining lemon and the butter to the pan. Allow the butter to melt and add the cream and a pinch of salt and pepper. Increase the heat and allow the sauce to bubble for a few seconds. Serve the fish with the sauce, lemon garnish, buttered new potatoes and vegetables of your choice.

David Shaw
The Schoolhouse Restaurant
John O' Groats (pictured)

herrings in oatmeal
for breakfast, lunch or dinner!

SERVES 6 for breakfast, 3-4 as a main dish
12 fresh herring fillets
6 oz/175g oatmeal
Salt and pepper
Fat or oil for frying

Mix a teaspoon of salt with the oatmeal and coat the herring fillets on both sides. Have frying pan ready with the fat smoking hot. Put herrings, in skin side uppermost and season. Fry the fish for 3 minutes each side. Drain on absorbent paper.

Delicious served for breakfast. For a main dish, serve with mashed potatoes and peas or more traditionally with potatoes boiled in their skins.

Etta Macleod

The first catch of the day – a fishing boat leaves Scrabster harbour

plaice in vermouth sauce

SERVES 4

4 fillets plaice
6 oz/150g butter
6 tablespoons dry vermouth
1 teaspoon tomato purée

Salt and pepper
1 small carton cream
Fresh parsley, chopped

Roll up the fillets and arrange in a buttered casserole. Melt butter, then add vermouth and tomato purée, stir, and add to casserole. Bake in a preheated oven at 200°C/400°F/Gas 6 for 30 minutes, or until the fish flakes when touched with a fork. Add cream and shake vigorously. Sprinkle with the parsley and serve. A lovely easy dish!

Sheila Farley-Sutton

kedgeree
a breakfast not quite fit for a President!

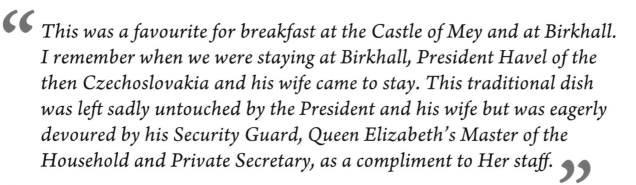

This was a favourite for breakfast at the Castle of Mey and at Birkhall. I remember when we were staying at Birkhall, President Havel of the then Czechoslovakia and his wife came to stay. This traditional dish was left sadly untouched by the President and his wife but was eagerly devoured by his Security Guard, Queen Elizabeth's Master of the Household and Private Secretary, as a compliment to Her staff.

14 oz/400g salmon cooked, skinned,
  boned and flaked
4 hard-boiled eggs, sliced
2 teacups cooked rice

5 oz/125g butter, cut into small squares
3-4 tablespoons cream
Salt and pepper

Mix ingredients together and warm in a preheated (170°C/325°F/Gas 3) oven.

David McMicking

salmon mousseline with a lobster sauce

1¼ lb/567g fresh salmon
6 egg whites
3 tablespoons lemon juice
¾ pint/450ml double cream
1 teaspoon anchovy essence

For the lobster sauce (makes 1 pint/600ml)
1 small lobster, cooked
¾ pint/450ml rich fish stock
½ pint/300ml double cream
3 tablespoons butter
3 tablespoons flour

Remove bones and skin from salmon. Chill. Place 2 of the egg whites in blender, add salmon and lemon juice, and season with salt and pepper and a teaspoon of anchovy essence. Blend at low speed to form a smooth paste. Put purée into a bowl and cool for a few hours in the fridge. Whip cream and whisk into fish purée. Beat the remaining egg whites and gently fold into mixture. Pour mixture into a large buttered soufflé dish or ramekin dishes. Stand in a bain-marie and bake in a preheated (150°C/300°F/Gas 2) oven for 45 to 60 minutes for the large dish, or approximately 30 minutes for the ramekins. Remove from the oven and leave to stand for 3 to 4 minutes before turning out onto a plate.

To make the sauce, shell the lobster and chop the meat. Set aside. Chop the shell and add to the fish stock and boil slowly for 20 minutes. Melt the butter and then add the flour, stirring until smooth. Add fish stock slowly after straining, then add the cream, and continue to cook until sauce is reduced to the desired consistency. Add the chopped lobster meat to the sauce, warm through and then pour over the mousseline(s) to serve.

Countess of Dalhousie

Wicked Chips

It must have been a Friday lunch as fish was on the menu. We were having a pre-lunch drink, and as it was nearly the weekend I had opted for a G&T. The Queen Mother suddenly stated that I had some 'wicked' socks on! It must have been my young officer phase as I had red socks on with my pinstripe suit. Having nearly choked on my gin, I enquired as to where Her Majesty had learnt such a word. Apparently Prince Harry had recently returned from Eton saying the new word was 'wicked' and Her Majesty had found this highly amusing, especially as it was followed by a hand gesture to reinforce it, which She promptly stood up and demonstrated. As the fish and potato wedges (not sure we were allowed to call them chips) were served by William Tallon, Her Majesty piped up, "Wicked, it's chips for lunch!"

William de Rouet

Shells in the Hall at
the Castle of Mey

mackerel ceviche

The seas around the Scottish coast teem with shoals of mackerel from mid-June until early October. It always surprises me that a lot of people take great delight in catching them but then cannot be bothered to eat them. Freshly filleted and fried in a little butter and oatmeal and served with a squeeze of lemon or a gooseberry sauce, I think that they are incomparable.

A somewhat more adventurous way of dealing with them is to create a ceviche. After a very successful afternoon's mackerel fishing with Rob Gordon at Barisdale on the north of the Knoydart Peninsula a few years ago, we had too many for supper. I volunteered to make a ceviche which effectively gave us another day to enjoy the mackerel, for unless they are absolutely fresh, they are not half so good.

First, fillet your mackerel and then slice off the skin. Chop them up into 1 inch/2.5cm pieces and put the flesh in a non-metallic bowl. For a main course allow a mackerel of about 1 lb/450g per person: for a starter half that quantity should be enough. Finely dice half an onion (preferably red to make it look more interesting) per person and squeeze enough of equal quantities of lemons and limes to cover the flesh. If you have a couple of mild red or green chillies and a couple of cloves of garlic finely dice them; if not a dash or two of Tabasco will do. Leave the mixture in the fridge for a couple of hours and then give it a good stir. The flesh will turn from translucent to white as the acid from the lemons and limes 'cooks' the fish.

Leave the mixture in the fridge for up to 24 hours and then serve with chopped parsley, buttered brown bread and a salad (avocado and tomatoes work particularly well).

Ashe Windham

lobster omelette thermidor

SERVES 4
1 1½ lb/500-600g cooked lobster
1 oz/20g finely chopped shallots
4 floz/114 ml white wine
8 eggs plus 2 egg yolks
5 tablespoon thermidor sauce
1 tablespoon whipped cream
¼ oz/5g (approx) chopped parsley
Salt and pepper

Place the white wine and shallots into a pan and reduce until dry. Remove the lobster meat from the shell, clean the meat and roughly dice.

Add the lobster to the shallots and warm through. Place approximately 1 tablespoon of thermidor sauce into the lobster and bind together, adjust seasoning.

Place remaining thermidor sauce into a separate pan. Mix in the egg yolks and chopped parsley. Fold in the whipped cream and adjust the seasoning.

Make four omelettes using 2 eggs per person. Divide the lobster mix equally between the omelettes. To serve, spread enough thermidor sauce over the top of each omlette (not too much otherwise your omelette will collapse).

Derek Quelch

dishwasher salmon

SERVES 8
5-7 lb/3-4kg whole salmon
Salt and pepper
2 oz/50g butter

Clean fish thoroughly. Season well inside with salt and pepper, the lemon, herbs of your choice and half the butter. WRAP UP VERY WELL in buttered tin foil using the rest of the butter. It must be totally sealed so be generous with your foil and use an extra thick kind if possible.

Place on top rack of your empty dishwasher, set temperature to hot, DO NOT ADD ANY DISHWASHER POWDER, and turn machine on in usual way to complete a full cycle. No short economy runs and leave until totally cold. RESULT: one delicious salmon steam-cooked to perfection irrespective of its size.

NOTE: This really does work and if you are catering for a large number you can cook two at a time while cooking others in a conventional fish kettle.

Christina Murray

salmon baked with coriander and orange

SERVES 4

4 salmon steaks
Mixture of crushed coriander seeds, red and black
   peppercorns (2 coriander to 1 peppercorn)
Fish stock

5 floz/150ml white wine
3 floz/75ml cream
Orange juice
Fresh coriander leaves

Put steaks in a foil-lined baking tray. Sprinkle with coriander/peppercorn mixture, pour fish stock and orange juice around salmon. Cover with foil. Bake in hot oven 200°C/400°F/Gas 9 for 15 to 20 minutes. Once cooked, remove steaks and reduce fish stock in pan. Add wine and cream. Reduce again. Add few coriander leaves and check seasoning. Add knob of butter to thicken. Serve the sauce around salmon on plate.

Sue Jenkins

Fresh out of the dishwasher!

Mussels on the rocks at Dunnet Beach.
Knowing what the tide is doing is essential
when collecting them!

mussels a la créme

The coast of the North of Scotland is littered with mussels. The trick is to dial up the tide timetable on the internet and select a piece of coastline which is accessible at very low tide but does not have too sandy a beach in the vicinity, for the mussels will have small pearls in them if collected from a sandy beach. The East end of Dunnet Beach is a very good spot!

I gave up bothering with the traditional method of creating Moules Marinière years ago, for it is altogether too much like hard work, what with trimming beards and scraping barnacles off the shells. Simply put the mussels into a large saucepan with just enough boiling water to cover them and then bring them back to a rolling boil with the lid on and let them simmer for no more than 3 minutes. You can tell when they are ready as the shells will have opened. Take them off the heat and discard the water and any mussels that haven't opened, leaving the mussels in the sink for them to cool. Meanwhile, prepare the sauce by frying a couple of onions and a couple of cloves of garlic in 1-2 oz/ 25-50g of butter. When the onions are translucent, add a pinch of turmeric and milled black pepper, a dash of Martini or white wine and a slug of cream. Mix the sauce together and leave to one side. The mussels will have cooled down sufficiently for you to take them out of their shells – pull off the beards at this point and pop the mussels into a couple of ramekins. If you find a sandy mussel, rinse it under the tap. Pour the sauce over them and put a layer of breadcrumbs over the top. Ten minutes before you are ready to eat, put the ramekins into a hot oven (200°C/400°F/ Gas 6) for 10 minutes and hey presto!

Ashe Windham

vegetables

hungarian lesco
a versatile sauce made with tomatoes and peppers

2 small red onions
2 lb/900g mixed peppers
2½ lb/1kg tomatoes
4 tablespoons olive oil
3 teaspoons sweet paprika
1 teaspoon salt
1 teaspoon hot paprika paste

Skin and finely chop the majority (approximately 2 lb/900g) of the tomatoes. Skin and slice the rest. De-core the peppers, remove the seeds and cut into 1 in/2.5cm squares and finely chop the onions.

Sauté the onions in the oil over a medium heat until golden brown. Put to the side and stir in the paprika; it is important to do this with the pan off the heat. Add the chopped tomatoes immediately to stop the paprika from burning. Add a bit of salt and cook over a low heat for 25 minutes. It is ready when the tomato and onions reduce to a thick paste.

Add the peppers and a little more salt and cook over a low heat for about 10 more minutes; then add the remaining sliced tomatoes. Continue cooking until the peppers are tender. Stir occasionally but do not cover or the steam will detach the skin from the peppers. Finish by adding the hot paprika paste.

This dish can be served with rice, mashed potatoes or noodles or as a sauce for meat dishes (see Hungarian Pork Fillet on p. 63). This dish also freezes well.

Ann Baird

arancini with a tomato sauce

For the arancini
1 coffee cup of Italian rice per person
½ a large onion, chopped very finely
Butter and olive oil
Saffron
Glass of white wine
Vegetable stock
Mozzarella cheese
Beaten egg
Fine breadcrumbs
Finely grated Parmesan
Flour, for dusting
Sunflower oil

For the tomato sauce
1 onion
1 carrot
1 stick celery
2 cloves garlic
Olive oil
2 tins Italian peeled plum tomatoes
Pinch of sugar
Salt and pepper
Stem of basil

Make a risotto by gently cooking the onion in a little butter and olive oil until soft and transparent. Add the rice and stir until it is coated with oil. Raise the heat and add the glass of white wine and stir until absorbed. Gradually add the hot stock, stirring all the time. Continue to add the stock, a ladle at a time, until the rice is nearly cooked. Add the saffron. When the rice is cooked remove it from heat and add a good piece of butter and plenty of finely grated Parmesan.

Transfer the rice into a dish and leave to cook down overnight. The next day take a large tablespoon of rice at a time and form into small balls. Into the centre of each ball put a small piece of mozzarella. Reform the balls and lightly flour. Roll in the beaten egg and then in the breadcrumbs. Refrigerate until needed.

To make the tomato sauce, finely chop the onion, carrot, celery and garlic and gently fry in olive oil until soft and transparent. Add the tinned tomatoes, with a pinch of sugar, salt and pepper and basil and cook over a medium heat, lid on, for about 1 hour or until well thickened and reduced. Season to taste and either sieve or liquidise if you want a smoother sauce.

To cook the arancini, deep fry in sunflower oil until golden. Serve with the hot tomato sauce, deep-fried parsley and plenty of finely grated Parmesan.

Olga Polizzi

131

The Queen Mother in one of Her favourite spots, the Shell Garden

The Shell Garden

It was another beautiful Mey morning when I said to Chef, "I won't be long, I'm going to get some tatties from the garden." I entered the garden through the little green wooden door and couldn't resist the call of the Shell Garden on the right. "Just one lucky Buckie*," I thought as I sifted through a few shells. Ten minutes later, the door opened and Beverly, another chef, came to join me. "Chef was wondering where you were," she said as we both hunted a Buckie. A few moments later the door opened and Joanna our other chef came to tell us that Chef was wondering where we both were, as she helped us find a Buckie. Soon the garden door burst open and in came Chef with our daily lady Helen, wanting to see what we were up to.

It must have been a hilarious sight from the Castle, all those blue-checked bottoms in the air as we hunted for a Buckie for Chef.   Sadly no Buckie shells but we did remember the tatties!

*Groatie Buckie shells are found on the sandy beaches around Orkney and Caithness. They are a token of good fortune and much sought after.

Sue Collings

creamed mey potatoes

2 lb/1kg potatoes
2 medium onions
2oz/50g butter
1 pint/600ml double cream
Salt and pepper

Peel and thinly slice potatoes, peel and thinly slice onions. Use half of the butter to grease dish, layer potatoes and onions alternately in dish, salt and pepper each layer, pour cream down the side (not over the top), dot with butter and cover with foil.

Place on middle shelf of oven 190°C/375°F/Gas 5 for 30 minutes, remove foil and cook until potatoes are soft. Great with roast Mey Lamb! (See recipe on page 56.)

Sue Collings
Sue Collings, a chef to Her Majesty The Queen Mother, says her memories of the Castle of Mey are "forever in my memory and my heart as Mey simply does that."

Champagne and Artichokes

Globe artichokes from the kitchen garden were regularly on the menu at the Castle of Mey. To guests who were encountering them for the first time, they might have seemed a little intimidating but Queen Elizabeth would give a step-by-step demonstration on how to dissect the artichoke and discard the inedible fuzzy part (called the "choke") covering the artichoke heart. Once everyone had finished Queen Elizabeth would encourage Her guests to take a sip of water which, She said, after eating an artichoke, tasted like Champagne – and She was right!

Richard Jenkins

focaccia with red onion and pepper

"My husband and I have been staying with Helen Hamilton at the House of Corsback near Dunnet for forty years and love both Caithness and the Castle of Mey."

2 teaspoon dried yeast
10 floz/300ml warm water
1lb/450g strong flour
3 tablespoons olive oil
1½ teaspoon salt

For Topping
2 floz/50ml olive oil
1 small red pepper, finely sliced
1 red onion, finely sliced

Whisk yeast into warm water and leave for 5 minutes. Put flour, oil and salt in a bowl, add yeast and mix. Transfer to floured board and knead for 2 minutes. Return to floured bowl, cover and rest for 1 hour. Knead on floured board for 2 minutes, then rest for 5 minutes. Stretch dough into greased baking tin 8x12 in/20x30cm). Drizzle olive oil over surface and sprinkle on some finely sliced pepper and onion. Cover and rest for 40 minutes.

Cook in a hot oven preheated to 200°C/400°F/Gas 6 for about 30 minutes or until golden.

I make this initially in a food processor which kneads well.

Delia Findlay

135

Some of the inhabitants of the Castle of Mey Animal Centre

luxury cauliflower cheese

1 cauliflower	½ teaspoon mustard powder
1 tablespoon vegetable oil	1 pint/600ml milk
1 small red pepper	8 oz/225g mature cheddar cheese, grated
1 small leek	Salt & black pepper
2 oz/50g plain flour	1 tablespoon chopped parsley

Cut cauliflower into florets, cook in pan of boiling salted water for 5 minutes until tender. Slice leek, de-seed and slice pepper, fry for 5 minutes or until softened. Stir the flour and mustard into pan, cook gently for about 2 minutes, stirring constantly. Remove from heat and gradually blend in milk. Return to heat and bring to boil. Continue stirring until thickened. Stir in 6 oz/175g of the cheese and add parsley. Pre-heat grill and put cauliflower into an ovenproof dish. Pour cheese sauce over and sprinkle remaining cheese on top. Grill for 2 to 3 minutes. Depending on taste, more cheese can be used or different varieties. Particularly nice with stilton.

Joan Miller

sweet potatoes with apples

SERVES 6

1 lb/450g sweet potatoes	6 oz/150g soft brown sugar
1¼ lb/550g cooking apples	1 level teaspoon nutmeg
3 oz/75g butter	1 tablespoon lemon juice
1 level teaspoon salt	

Peel and thinly slice the sweet potatoes. Peel, core and thinly slice the apples. Butter a casserole dish and arrange alternate layers of sweet potatoes and apples, starting and finishing with sweet potatoes. Sprinkle each layer with salt, sugar, nutmeg and lemon juice, and dot with the remaining butter. Set casserole on the lowest shelf of an oven pre-heated to 200°C/400°F/Gas 6 and cook for 40 minutes or until the potatoes are tender. Serve straight from the casserole.

Christina Murray

maggie's baked spinach

SERVES 6

3 lb/1.3kg spinach, tough stalks removed
2 eggs
14 floz/400ml double cream

4 oz/100g Parmesan, freshly grated
½ teaspoon grated nutmeg
Sea salt and freshly ground black pepper

Preheat the oven to 190°C/375°F/Gas 5. Beat the eggs and cream together for 1 minute in a large bowl. Add the Parmesan, nutmeg and pepper and salt. Blanch the spinach in plenty of boiling salted water for 1 minute, and drain well (I steam it). Chop roughly and mix well with the egg and cream mixture. Pour into a medium-sized baking dish – the mixture should not be less than 1½ in/4cm deep. Place uncovered in the top of the preheated oven for 30 minutes. (I do about 20 minutes in top right Aga of a 4-oven Aga.) Serve hot. The top should be crisp, while the underneath should still be slightly creamy.

Day Howden

artichoke penne

SERVES 4

10 oz/250g penne pasta
1 jar artichoke hearts, quartered
4 oz/100g pine kernels, toasted
5 oz/125g baby leeks, washed and chopped

6 cloves garlic, chopped (less if preferred)
4 tablespoons olive oil
4 oz/100g Parmesan, freshly grated

Cook the penne pasta in boiling water with a dash of salt. Lightly fry the baby leeks and garlic in a little of the olive oil.

Drain the cooked penne and place in a large bowl. Add the quartered artichokes, toasted pine kernels, cooked leeks, garlic and the olive oil and toss well. Serve immediately with the grated Parmesan.

Lili Panagi

139

ellwood pantry peas

> " *While we were at Mey we often got a request from upstairs via a footman for the peas, which came in copious amounts from the garden. These would be duly returned by a Lady-in-Waiting all shucked, with pods on the top to stop them drying out. Glorious entertainment by the fire.* "
>
> **Sue Collings**

8 oz/225g peas (frozen or fresh)
2 medium onions
8 rashers of bacon
2 oz/50g butter
2 tablespoons of Parmesan cheese, grated

Finely dice onions and fry in butter until soft. Cut bacon into small pieces and fry in a little oil until golden brown and crisp. Place peas into pan, add water and heat (frozen) or cook until tender (fresh).

Drain peas and place in frying pan with onions and add bacon to pan, mix and place in serving dish or on plate and dust with the cheese.

Perfect with pork chops and boiled potatoes.

John Collings
John and Sue Collings used to run a catering business called Ellwood Pantry when they first went down to live in Dorset

The Garden at Mey in
the early evening sun

tomato summer pudding

½ in/1¼cm slices of bread, with crusts cut off, sufficient to line a 2½ pint/1½ litre bowl
4 large chopped tomatoes
2 oz/50g chopped sundried tomatoes
1 lb/500g passata

1 jar antipasto artichokes, drained
4 chopped spring onions
3 oz/75g chopped olives
1 tablespoon mixed herbs
1 handful of fresh torn basil leaves

Line the bottom and the sides of a bowl with slices of bread, allowing them to overlap. Mix all the other ingredients together and season well. Add the mix to the bowl, packing it well down as you go. Cover with more slices of bread and then with cling film. Put a weighted plate on top and then leave in the fridge for 24 hours. When ready to serve turn out the pudding and serve with salad.

Ann Baird

parsnips molly parkin

a meal in itself

2 lb/1kg parsnips
1 lb/1kg tomatoes, skinned and sliced
3 oz/75g butter
½ pint/300ml single or double cream
3 tablespoons soft brown sugar

Salt and pepper
6 oz/150g grated Gruyère (or whatever cheese you have)
4 rounded tablespoons breadcrumbs

Peel and slice parsnips, or cut into thinnish fingers, and boil or steam slightly. Grease casserole. Layer parsnips in the dish, then sprinkle with the sugar, salt, pepper and cream. Continue layering with the tomatoes and cheese, then start again. Sprinkle the breadcrumbs on top and dot with butter. Put in a preheated slow oven at 150°C/300°F/Gas 2 for 40 minutes.

Day Howden

roast parsnips with honey and thyme
an ordinary vegetable made special

1 lb/450g parsnips, peeled
1-2 tablespoons clear honey
1 tablespoon oil
1 tablespoon finely chopped fresh thyme
Salt and pepper

Heat oven to 190°C/375°F/Gas 5. Mix honey and oil together. Put parsnips in a tray, coat with honey and oil. Sprinkle with thyme, salt and pepper.

Bake for about 1 hour. Sprinkle with fresh thyme before serving.

Lance Purcell

corn pudding
an old family recipe from Canada

14 oz/400g can of creamed style sweetcorn
2 eggs
2 oz/50g sugar

5 floz/120ml milk
2-3 tablespoons butter

Beat eggs and add sugar and milk. Melt butter in a shallow baking dish in the oven or a microwave. Add creamed corn to egg mixture and stir. Pour into a baking dish with melted butter and bake in a moderate oven (170°C/325°F/Gas 3) for about 1 hour.

This is an old family recipe and one that children especially enjoy. It is served as a vegetable dish and is especially wonderful with chicken or turkey. It is served every Christmas in our home.

Sarah Jane Dumbrille

"I am a Canadian living in a small village called Maitland on the banks of the St Lawrence River in Eastern Ontario, one hour south of Ottawa. My family and I had a dream come true this past June when we had an opportunity to visit the Castle of Mey. Touched by what we saw, we became Friends."

The table in the Dining Room at Mey with the Victorian cranberry glass bells.

Dining at the Castle of Mey

The dining room table at the Castle of Mey had sets of candelabra at each end and every candle had its own candle shade. The shades had been painted with pictures of country cottages and each cottage window had been carefully cut out so that, when the candles were lit, the cottage lights also gleamed out. The result was delightful.

Queen Elizabeth had a set of Victorian cranberry glass bells next to Her by the table, each with its own chime, which She rang during dinner to signify the end of the course to the staff.

Richard Jenkins

Mary Ann's Cottage

This croft, preserved now by the Caithness Heritage Trust for people to visit and enjoy, was built in 1850 by Mary Ann Calder's grandfather at Dunnet Bay and was worked by three generations of the same family. Queen Elizabeth, sadly, due to illness, could not 'open' this fascinating window onto our crofting past, which She had been instrumental in preserving. However, as soon as She was better, Queen Elizabeth visited the Cottage, and during Her tour was shown the 'charm stone' for healing animals which was wrapped up in an old laddered Lisle stocking, just as Mary Ann had kept it. Queen Elizabeth's first remark was that She had not seen a Lisle stocking since the War. She unwrapped it and then held the stone before moving it from hand to hand. Bunty Gunn, who then chaired the Trust, asked Her whether it made Her feel better. With that wonderful smile She started to dance and said, "By the minute. By the minute."

The Earl of Caithness

parsnip drop scones with apple sauce

4 large parsnips
2.2 lb/1kg Bramley apples
12 oz/350g self raising flour
Sugar to taste
4 eggs, beaten

Milk
1 Savoy cabbage, thinly sliced
Salt and pepper
6-8 (per person) chestnuts
Nutmeg (optional)

Peel and core parsnips. Cook in boiling salted water until soft. Mash and leave to cool. Mix flour, eggs and enough milk to make a thick batter. Add the mashed parsnips and season with salt and pepper, and nutmeg, if desired. Heat enough butter to cover the bottom of a frying pan until hot and then add the mixture, the size of a saucer, in batches. Cook until golden brown, turning once and adding more butter, if required. Keep warm. Meanwhile, blanch and stir-fry the cabbage in a little seasoned butter. Serve a scone on each warmed plate, with a dollop of warm apple sauce (the apples stewed with sugar to taste) on top, and pile on the cabbage with the roughly chopped chestnuts mixed in. Delicious!

Edward Murray

austrian soured cream cabbage

1 small cabbage (Savoy is best)
2 onions
2 tablespoons butter

¼ pint/150ml soured cream
Paprika
Salt and pepper

Chop cabbage and onion finely. Toss onion in butter until slightly softened, then add the cabbage and stir until the butter coats it. Add the paprika, salt and pepper and soured cream. Put into a slow preheated oven (150°C/300°F/Gas 2) in a dish with a lid on for half an hour. Adding some pieces of crispy fried bacon makes this even more delicious.

Day Howden

beetroot gratin

4-6 large cooked beetroots, skinned
3 oz/90g Strathdon blue cheese, crumbled

Sea salt and freshly ground black pepper
¼ pint/150ml single cream

Chop the beetroot. Preheat oven to 200°C/400°F/Gas 6. Butter a gratin dish and sprinkle some of the cheese on the bottom. Place half the beetroot in the dish, add more cheese, then the remaining beetroot, the rest of the cheese and seasoning. Pour in the cream and bake for 15 minutes.

Christina Murray

A fine specimen of a cabbage
in the walled garden at Mey

puddings
& savouries

Glamis House Summer Pudding
(see recipe on page 162)

chocolate cream sophie

" The extraordinary thing about this simple pudding is that people always ask what the secret ingredient is or what alcohol has been used. The answer to both is none! "

SERVES 6-8

4 oz/100g brown breadcrumbs
4 oz/100g demerara sugar
8 teaspoons cocoa powder

4 teaspoons coffee powder
¾ pint/450ml double cream

Stir together coffee, cocoa, crumbs and sugar. Whip cream into soft peaks (not too stiff or it becomes difficult to layer). Layer in a large glass bowl, starting with crumb mixture and ending with a layer of the cream. Decorate with grated chocolate or crumbled flake or homemade chocolate rose leaves.

Note: At Christmas I start with a layer of sweetened chestnut purée at the bottom of the bowl (to which I might add a teaspoon of brandy).

The Hon. Mrs Nicolson

steamed marmalade pudding

SERVES 6-8

3 eggs
6 oz/150g caster sugar
6 oz/150g selfraising flour, sifted

6 oz/150g butter
3 tablespoons marmalade (see recipe on p. 206)

Cream the butter and sugar together. Stir 1 tablespoon of the marmalade into the mixture. Add the eggs one by one, beating them into the butter and sugar mixture. Fold in the flour. Grease a medium-sized 1½-2 pint/1 litre pudding basin and place the remaining marmalade in the bottom. Add the sponge mixture to the basin. Cover with greased parchment paper and tin foil, pleated across the centre to allow for rising and secure tightly with string tied under the lip of the basin. Steam for 1 to 1½ hours. Serve with marmalade sauce (4 tablespoons marmalade and 1 tablespoon of water, heated gently until runny) and custard or fresh cream. This recipe can also be made with jam, or the grated zest of 2 lemons.

Michael Sealey

stornaway clootie dumpling
cooked in a cloth called a 'clootie'

1½ lb/675g self raising flour
8 oz/225g raisins
8 oz/225g sultanas
6 oz/175g brown sugar
6 oz/175g shredded suet
3 teaspoons mixed spice
3 teaspoons cinnamon
2 teaspoons bicarbonate of soda
2 teaspoons baking powder

3 tablespoons treacle
½ pint/300ml – ¾ pint/425ml milk
2 large eggs

(You will also need a large pan of boiling water, a side plate to put underneath the dumpling in the pan, a square of cloth (approx 24 in x 30 in/60cm x 76cm) and a length of string.)

Mix all the dry ingredients together. Add treacle, eggs and milk, and mix with a wooden spoon until well blended. Scald the cloth briefly in boiling water, ring out well and dredge with a little flour. Turn the mixture on to the cloth. Dredge lightly again with the flour to prevent the cloth from sticking when the dumpling is cooked. Tie securely with string making sure there are no loose ends and leaving enough room to allow the mixture to swell (a finger width between the mixture and the string is a good guide). Place the dumpling on the plate in the large pan of boiling water. Boil steadily for 3½ to 4 hours, topping up the level with more boiling water as required. Carefully lift the dumpling on to a plate and remove the cloth. Invert dumpling on to a large plate and fully remove the cloth. Leave to dry naturally for 20 to 30 minutes. Enjoy!

Serve warm with cream or custard, cold with butter or fried with bacon and egg.

Etta Macleod

jam puffs

" *I remember the marvellous picnic lunches that would await us after a good morning's walk on the hill and at which Queen Elizabeth was always present. At one we were given delicious jam puffs. Being the newest guest I was instructed what I had to do. I had to eat it in my fingers and firstly bite off a corner before pouring in the cream. I then had to eat it making as little mess as possible. There was a great deal of laughter from everyone else as the cream firstly ran out over my hands and then dripped on to whatever was below. I just hoped that another new guest would arrive soon to complete the challenge!* **"**

The Earl of Caithness

Sheet or block of thinly rolled puff pastry (homemade is better)
Homemade jam or marmalade (see recipe on page 206)
Sweet mincemeat is good at Christmas
1 egg, beaten
Icing sugar

(You will also need a 2 in/5cm plain round pastry cutter,
a 3 in/8cm fluted round pastry cutter and a baking sheet.)

Cut the required amount of pastry discs with large cutter; place a small amount of chosen filling in the centre of each one. Lightly brush with beaten egg and fold to form a half moon. Use finger and thumb to crimp round the edges, then use the small plain cutter to gently seal the parcel, this leaves a nice neat line – don't prick the top as this will let the filling out. Bake on middle shelf at 180°C/350°F/Gas 4 until golden brown.

Remove and dust lightly with icing sugar, place under a hot grill to glaze. Watch carefully as this will not take long – as we used to say, what's black and smoky and lives under the grill?!

Sue Collings

bread and butter toffee pudding

" This is one of my most asked-for recipes – try it and you'll see why! It's extremely easy and perfect for weekend and shooting lunches. I haven't included quantities as this depends on numbers, but allow two slices of bread per person and serve with lots of cream. "

Make the sauce by simmering together one third each of the butter, brown sugar and golden syrup.

Divide slices of thick white decrusted bread in three. Cover the bottom of an ovenproof dish with the sauce and lay a layer of the bread 'fingers' on top of the sauce.

Soak the remaining bread lightly in milk, cover with more sauce and continue for two layers until final layer of sauce. Bake in a preheated oven at 170°C/325°F/Gas 3 until custard is set and top is chewy and golden.

For added interest, intersperse a layer of mushed-up cooking apple.

Lady Edmonstone

154

fruit mousse

"This is my favourite pudding for a party as it never fails to please and freezes well without the decoration."

SERVES 6-8

½ pint/300ml liquidised purée of any soft fruit
3 eggs, separated
1 packet (3 teaspoons) gelatine
4 oz/100g caster sugar
½ pint/300ml double or whipping cream
5 floz/120ml warm water or fruit juice

Liquidise the fruit into a purée (if using frozen fruit melt in a pan with a little water and sugar). Fruit with pips needs to be put through a sieve. Beat the egg yolks with the sugar until pale and creamy. Dissolve the gelatine in water or juice. Add the purée to the egg and sugar mixture. Add the gelatine and stir. Whisk the cream (but not too stiff) and fold in as well. Lastly whisk the egg white until stiff and fold in. Put in dish in fridge to set. Decorate with whipped cream piped peaks, crumbled meringues and/or fruit as appropriate.

Jane Walker-Okeover

chocolate roulade
a gluten-free pudding

SERVES 6-8

5 egg yolks
5 egg whites
3 tablespoons cocoa
4 oz/100g icing sugar

½ pint/300ml whipped cream (flavoured, if desired, with a dash of marsala or brandy and 1 tablespoon of icing sugar)

Beat egg yolks until thick, add the sugar and beat again thoroughly. Add cocoa powder. Beat again. Fold in stiffly beaten egg whites. Spread on a baking tray (8 in x 12 in/20cm x 30cm) lined with lightly oiled baking parchment. Bake at 180°C/350°F/Gas 4 for 10 minutes. Turn out on to a piece of baking parchment dusted with icing sugar. Gently peel back the parchment. When cool spread with whipped cream (add marsala and icing sugar, if desired, before whipping). Roll gently from the long side. This can sometimes crack but that is part of the look of the roulade and can easily be improved with a dusting of icing sugar just before serving!

Felicity Colville

A Diary Entry

Saturday 22 August 1998: Ashe Windham invited me to the Castle of Mey to meet the Trustees of the Queen Elizabeth Castle of Mey Trust and to have lunch with Queen Elizabeth. On arriving the Equerry, William de Rouet, Irish Guards, greeted me and took me up to the drawing room and later we all went up the tower to see the view. Here was the flagpole with the Standard flying, half Royal, half Bowes-Lyon. From there one could see to Orkney and also to the walled garden.

We then went down to the walled garden, which is lovely, lots of high box, vegetables and flowers, all of which have to be ready when Queen Elizabeth is here. Circling, we came to another garden, one much favoured by The Prince of Wales, evidently. Here were lovely cowslips which rare beams of sunlight can strike.

We returned to the Castle and around 12.30 Queen Elizabeth came in. She wore a pale blue woollen suit with a tweed lapel, two strings of pearls and a small double sapphire and diamond brooch. She walked with Her stick, but looked intensely alert – tiny, of course, but very bright eyed. You would never have the slightest idea that She was 98. Queen Elizabeth sat in a high chair and I sat next to Her. We had a long talk, first about restoring houses. She said that She had been so pleased to rescue this Castle as it was about to be pulled down. She'd never been to this part of the world before staying with Clare Vyner. He lived at the House of the Northern Gate.

Presently we went in to lunch. I was seated between Ashe and Arabella Windham. I should have mentioned that William [Tallon] was there. He was first to be seen in a bright turquoise vest and then later he put on his dark blue livery with the red "ER"s on it. He was very friendly and put opposite me an ashtray with The Queen Mother's head on it and the wrong Coronation Date – Oct. 2 1937. Evidently She bought these for fun.

I observed The Queen Mother occasionally at lunch, sitting under the great woven coat of arms. At one point, as the sun came round and shone through one of the side windows She put on dark glasses. We had a good egg and lobster dish [oeufs drumkilbo] and then lamb with roast potatoes and heavy vegetables. White wine was served with the first course, claret with the second. A very rich roly-poly pudding with golden syrup followed and then by cheese, coffee and port. William was, as ever, wickedly zealous in recharging the glasses.

On saying goodbye, The Queen Mother asked me to stay a moment and we had a further chat. Amazing, above all else, was that She was so alert, so interested, so outgoing. Also quite funny and saying what She wanted.

Hugo Vickers

View towards the Orkneys
from the Castle Tower

lavender meringues

Makes approximately 12 merigues

2 large egg whites
5 oz/125g caster sugar

1 teaspoon white vinegar
1 rounded teaspoon dried lavender

Whisk egg whites until fairly stiff. Add sugar, and gradually fold in vinegar and lavender. Spoon or pipe on to baking trays lined with parchment paper. Cook for 1½ to 2 hours in a preheated over at 130°C/250°F/Gas ½ until crisp. Serve with whipped cream and fruit.

Lance Purcell

meringue roulade

" *This is impressive looking and delicious – one of life's star recipes. Once you have mastered the art of rolling it up it will be your friend for life! The meringue alone freezes immaculately (or with a lemon curd filling) so you can make any number in advance for a larger party – I once froze fifteen!* "

Allow 12 oz/350g caster sugar and 6 egg whites per 12 people. Whip the whites until softly dry and then continue whipping, slowly adding dessertspoons of the sugar until wonderfully thick and glossy (longer than you think). Spread into a rectangle roughly 12 in x 8 in/30cm x 20cm on waxed (or special) baking paper laid on a baking sheet. Peak up with the flat of a palette knife to look pretty. Bake for approximately 5 minutes in a moderate oven until peaks are brownish and then reduce to a low oven temperature for approximately 30 minutes (wedge open the top left Aga door with a wedge of paper to let the steam escape).

Invert on to another waxed sheet and spread with whipped cream mixed with some vanilla yoghurt, top with any filling you fancy from fruit to chocolate (I seem to gravitate to mangos and raspberries). Score across width with a pointed knife to help initial rolling up.

Starting with a mixture of your fingers and holding the waxed paper at the short end, create a tight roll of the roulade. Holding the edge of the paper continue rolling it up until you get to the end and then holding it in the 'cradle' of the paper transfer decisively on to a smart serving platter – squish into a better shape by gently pressing hands along length and at both ends. Be brave!

Lady Edmonstone

Lavender meringues made by Lance Purcell

A Much-Cherished Memory

In the summer of 1947 King George VI and Queen Elizabeth came to stay at Beaufort Castle, near Beauly, as guests of my uncle Shimi and aunt Rosie Lovat. Whilst only five years old I well remember the occasion because the nursery was full of young cousins and we were all very excited throughout the visit. Nanny Tansy tried to keep us under control with all sorts of threats of a smacking, but we all knew she didn't really mean it.

We heard that the King and Queen were going to attend some evening reception so we decided to sneak up the back stairs in our dressing gowns and get a preview. Somewhat cheekily we knocked on their bedroom door which to our surprise was answered by a Lady-in-Waiting. We asked if we could see the Queen's crown but the Lady-in-Waiting said that it was in London, however if we waited we could see something very similar. A few moments later, Queen Elizabeth came to the door wearing a long evening dress and a huge, beautiful, sparkling tiara. She spoke to us for a while as we stood gawping in the corridor before being gently shooed off by the Lady-in-Waiting.

Our covert mission was blown because we ran down the back stairs shouting, "We've seen the Queen's crown, we've seen the Queen's crown!". Nanny Tansy was not best pleased when we arrived back in the nursery!

Jeremy Phipps

Pictured: The Queen Mother dances with Viscount Thurso at a Silver Jubilee Ball in 1977

regency pudding

" This recipe originates from Lady Lovat and her cook, Joan Birnie. I have no idea if this was on the menu during the Royal visit but it is delicious! "

For the caramel
2 tablespoons water
3 oz/75g of granulated sugar
Pan of cold water
Enamel or tin plate and a 2½ pint/1½ltr metal mould

For the caramel sauce
1 egg
2-3 tablespoons cream

For the lemon soufflé cream
3 oz/75g butter
Grated zest and juice of a large lemon
6 tablespoons sugar
5 eggs, separated

For the caramel, boil the sugar and water in the mould over a moderate heat. Swirl the syrup around (do not stir it) until it finally goes toffee brown and begins to caramelise (best to wear oven gloves for this). When it is the right colour, dip the outside of the mould immediately in the pan of cold water for 2 to 3 seconds, to cool it slightly. Then, holding the mould firmly, tilt it in all directions to film over the bottom and insides completely with a thin coating of caramel. When the caramel has ceased to run turn the mould over a plate and set aside.

For the lemon soufflé, cream the butter and sugar, add the egg yolks and lemon and beat lightly over moderate heat until they become like thick cream. This is best done in a basin over a bain-marie. Take off the heat and cool. Beat the whites to a peaking froth and add to the lemon mixture when these are cool.

Spoon the lemon cream into the caramelised mould, cover it with the tin plate and put it into a large saucepan of very gently shuddering water, enough for it to come two-thirds up the side of the mould. The water around the mould must not boil. It should be ready in 40 to 50 minutes. Turn out on to a hot dish with caramel sauce poured around it.

The caramel sauce is easily made by pouring 1 beaten egg and two or three tablespoons of cream into the now empty mould, putting it back over a gentle heat and whisking hard so that the egg cream absorbs the last traces of caramel. Do not overheat or the egg will scramble.

Jeremy Phipps

a favourite glamis house summer pudding

1½ lb/675g mixed soft fruit (strawberries, raspberries, red and blackcurrants as well as black cherries are all suitable)

6-8 slices crustless white bread ½ in/1cm thick
4oz /100g caster sugar
(You will need a 1½ lb/675g pint basin)

Line the bottom of the basin with enough slices of bread to cover completely. Mould the rest to cover basin completely, overlapping if necessary, and cut to shape so that the bread fits closely together. Hull and wash the fruit (de-stone if necessary). Put the fruit in a wide heavy-based pan and sprinkle with the sugar. Bring to the boil over a very low heat and cook for 2 to 3 minutes only, until the sugar dissolves and the juices begin to run. Remove the pan from the heat and set aside 2 tablespoons of the juice. Spoon the fruit and remaining juice into the prepared basin and cover the surface with the remaining bread to form a lid.

Put a plate that fits inside the basin on top of the pudding and weigh it down with a heavy tin or jar. Leave in the fridge overnight. To serve, turn upside down on a plate to unmould and pour over the reserved juice. Serve with cream.

The Dowager Countess of Strathmore

glamis grape brûlée

" *This delicious pudding was a favourite with The Queen Mother when She visited Glamis, especially when the grapes were ripe in the greenhouse at the Castle. Glamis grapes were famous when She was young and won all the prizes at the Chelsea Flower Show.* "

Peel and de-seed about 1 lb/450g green grapes and place them in a fireproof flat dish. Whisk some double cream and cover the grapes. Place the dish in the refrigerator for 2 or 3 hours to stiffen the cream. Sprinkle 3 tablespoons of demerara sugar over the mixture and place under a hot grill, just long enough to caramelise the sugar. Turn the dish around, if necessary. Immediately replace in the refrigerator and leave for at least 3 hours until the cream is firm.

The Dowager Countess of Strathmore

In the 1860s Glamis estate came to the forefront of Victorian agricultural achievement. During this time a new Kitchen Garden was established as well as the glasshouses, where the prizewinning grapes were grown

tipsy tart

" This is my favourite South African recipe. All my diets have faltered each time I come into contact with this delicious pudding. It is called Cape Brandy Pudding in South Africa and is enjoyed with tea as a cake or after dinner as a pudding. I personally could have it for breakfast and lunch too! "

For the tart
4 oz/100g dates, chopped
¼ pint/150ml boiling water
1 teaspoon bicarbonate of soda
5 oz/125g butter, softened
8 oz/225g caster sugar
1 egg beaten
6 oz/150g plain flour
Walnuts, chopped

For the syrup
4 oz/100g sugar
3 tablespoons/50ml water
1 teaspoon butter
1 teaspoon vanilla essence
1 tablespoon /25ml brandy (and a drop
   more, to taste!)
(I double all the ingredients and use a large rectangular baking tray. I also add extra dates and walnuts)

For the tart, preheat the oven to 180°C/350°F/Gas 4 and grease an 8 in/20cm pie dish. Soak the dates in the bicarbonate of soda and boiling water until soft. Leave to cool, then strain.

Cream the butter and sugar together with the egg. Sift dry ingredients into mixture and fold in. Add dates and walnuts into the mixture.

Place the mixture into pie dish and bake for about 30 minutes or until skewer comes out clean.

For the syrup, dissolve the sugar into the water together on the stove and heat until the mixture has thickened a little. Remove from the stove and stir in the vanilla essence, butter and brandy. Pour the hot syrup over the warm tart and serve with cream or ice cream.

Jackie Johnstone

upside down pear and gingerbread pudding

SERVES 6

4 oz/100g butter
4 oz/100g soft brown sugar
15 oz/425g tin pears in fruit juice, drained and sliced
4 oz/100g plain flour
½ teaspoon bicarbonate of soda
2 teaspoons cinnamon
1 teaspoon ground ginger
Pinch nutmeg and ground cloves
1 egg, lightly beaten
4 oz/100g dark brown sugar

3 oz/75g treacle
¼ pint/150ml milk
double cream for serving

For the fudge sauce
4 oz/100g butter
6 oz/150g soft brown sugar
½ pint/300ml double cream
few drops vanilla essence

Make topping first by melting half of the butter and soft brown sugar. Stir for 1 to 2 minutes over a gentle heat. Pour into ovenproof dish (8 in/20cm diameter). Arrange sliced pears in fan shape over sauce. Sieve together into bowl the flour, bicarbonate of soda, cinnamon, ginger, nutmeg and cloves. Melt remaining butter and mix in egg, dark brown sugar, treacle and milk. Stir into dry ingredients and mix well. Spoon mixture over pears. Smooth surface and bake in a preheated over at 350°F/180°C/Gas 4 for 40-50 minutes. Remove from oven, leave to settle for 2 minutes and then turn out on to warm plate.

For the hot fudge sauce, place the butter, sugar and cream in a saucepan and heat gently until the butter is melted and sugar dissolved. Simmer sauce for 3 to 5 minutes, then add a few drops of vanilla essence.

Serve the pudding with the hot fudge sauce and cream.

Clare Macpherson-Grant Russell

soufflé de rothschild

> *James de Rothschild's Chef Careme was the greatest in Europe in the 1800s and he created several dishes for his patron. None was more suited to Rothschild's personality than the extravagant and indulgent Soufflé de Rothschild. 'Goldwasser' is a clear, 80 proof orange-anise flavoured liqueur containing small flakes of 22 or 23 carat gold leaf in suspension.*

4 tablespoons Goldwasser
4 oz/100g finely grated candied cherries
4 oz/100g sugar
Pinch of salt
2 oz/50g flour
15 floz/360ml half milk and half single cream
5 egg yolks
1 teaspoon vanilla
Butter
Granulated sugar
6 egg whites

Preheat oven to 200°C/400°C/Gas 6. Soak cherries in Goldwasser for 15 minutes. Set aside. Mix sugar, flour and salt together in a saucepan. Add cream and whisk over a low heat until mixture thickens. Remove from the heat.

Add a little of the heated sauce to the egg yolks, then whisk the yolk mixture into the remaining cream mixture. Add the vanilla, cherries, and Goldwasser. Let it cool to room temperature.

Butter 3 pint/1½ltr soufflé mould and sprinkle it with the sugar. Beat egg whites until they begin to froth. Gradually beat in 2 tablespoons of sugar until they form stiff peaks. Fold 10 floz/240ml of the egg whites into the custard. Then fold custard into remaining eggs whites. Fill the mould with custard mixture. Bake for 15 to 20 minutes or until the top of the soufflé is golden.

Christina Murray

A Surprise Pudding

Queen Elizabeth was always very interested in food and what She, Her household and guests ate. In pre-War tradition and in whichever of Her houses She was staying, which in turn depended on the time of year, the "menu book" was sent up to Her each day with suggestions and alternative choices for lunch and dinner and which were often amended by Her. Her chef went to see Her when She came downstairs in the morning.

I remember that on one occasion I gave a small luncheon party for Her at a London hotel. I had ordered the lunch beforehand and thought it would be fun to give The Queen Mother a surprise for the pudding; this was a Soufflé de Rothschild, a somewhat complicated and elaborate dish which is really far too rich, hence its name. The pudding appeared and unlike my other guests who were mystified, Queen Elizabeth immediately knew what it was and exclaimed, "OH! What a treat, I haven't seen this since we went to lunch with Philip Sassoon in Park Lane before the War!" Her memory was phenomenal.

John Bowes-Lyon

Looking over the Pentland Firth to the Island of Hoy

Castle of Mey sycamores in Spring

strawberry soufflé

SERVES 4

1 lb 2 oz/500g strawberries, hulled
6 oz/150g caster sugar
1 vanilla pod
2½ tablespoons cornflour

Softened butter, for greasing
4 egg whites
Sifted icing sugar

Preheat oven to 200°C/400°F/Gas 6. Take 4 soufflé dishes, 3½ in/9 cm diameter and 2½ in/6.5cm deep. Butter well and dust with a little caster sugar. To make the jam base, blend the strawberries with 4 oz/100g of the caster sugar to make a purée. Sieve into a heavy-bottomed saucepan. Scrape in the seeds from the vanilla pod and bring to the boil over a medium heat, whisking continuously. Mix the cornflour with 4 tablespoons of cold water and then whisk into the purée until it thickens. Cool and then chill.

Whisk the whites with the remaining caster sugar until they form soft peaks. Fold into the jam base and divide among the four soufflé dishes, filling to the top. Level with the back of a knife and bake for 9 to 11 minutes or until risen by half again. Dust with icing sugar and serve immediately.

Olga Polizzi

banana pudding

" This is a recipe I learnt from my aunt, Dame Joan Vickers, who was MP for Plymouth from 1955 to 1974. "

8-10 bananas
2 large tubs double cream
Milk Flake chocolate
Rum (to taste)
(All of these ingredients can be increased if a larger pudding is needed and you can add other things such as nuts or crushed strawberries, if desired)

Slice the bananas very thinly and put them in a glass bowl. Crumble up the Flake chocolate and scatter most of it over the bananas, saving just a bit for the top. Pour in the double cream.
Pour in some rum according to how alcoholic you want it to be. Stir it all up until you get a fairly rich, solid mixture. Put in the refrigerator, preferably overnight, but for at least 3 hours, so that it sets hard. Before serving, sprinkle the remaining Flake chocolate over the top to cover it. This will produce a delicious pudding and will take no longer than 10 minutes to make.

Hugo Vickers

canapés a la créme

" *This could be a starter but I prefer it as a delicious savoury.* **"**

SERVES 4

8 slices white bread
12 anchovy fillets
4 oz/100g butter

4 level tablespoons clotted cream
Fresh parsley to garnish

Cut rounds from each slice of bread with a 3 in/7.5cm cutter. Drain the anchovy fillets and cut each in half lengthways. Fry bread in butter till golden brown and keep warm. When ready to serve, arrange three anchovy fillets on each round of fried bread, spoon over the cream and garnish with the parsley. Serve quickly before the cream melts into the bread.

James Murray

scotch woodcock

" *An elegant but simple dish, it can be used as a first course or, as Her Majesty did, as a savoury instead of a pudding. The egg served in small bread baskets can be made in advance leaving you with stress-free entertaining.* **"**

SERVES 4

1 large white loaf, cut into 2 in/5cm-thick slices
6 large eggs
8 button mushrooms
2 oz/50g butter

2 tablespoons cream
Cooking oil
Salt and pepper

For the bread baskets, use a 2 in/5cm round cutter to cut 4 pieces (dipping the cutter in warm water helps make it easier as does twisting it). Use a smaller 1½ in/3.75cm cutter to score a circle inside the larger, only about half as deep. Heat some oil, test with a few crumbs to see if it is hot, place each basket scored-side down and fry until golden brown. Turn, repeat and drain on kitchen paper. Use a small knife to prise off the disc which is to become a lid, scoop out the insides to leave a shell and discard. Gently fry 2 button mushrooms for each basket and keep warm. Gently melt the butter in a small pan (do not brown). Mix the eggs, cream and seasoning together, and lightly scramble. Mound the egg into each basket, top with a lid and a mushroom or two and serve.

Sue Collings

baking

Chocolate cake served in the Drawing Room at Mey

burn o'vat rock cakes

> *These rock cakes are named after Burn O'Vat, a beauty spot close to Balmoral between Ballater and Aboyne. They were served to the Royal Family for teas and picnics in Scotland. Her Majesty Queen Elizabeth The Queen Mother used to say, being the perfect host, 'the men come in hungry'.*

8 oz/250g self raising flour
3 oz/75g butter or margarine
3 oz/75g sugar
3 oz/75g mixed dried fruit
1 oz/25g mixed chopped peel

1 teaspoon mixed spice
1 lightly beaten egg
2 tablespoons milk (approximately enough to
    bind the mixture)
Demerara sugar to decorate

Preheat the oven to 180°C/350°F/Gas 4.

Place flour and sugar in mixing bowl and rub in butter until it resembles sand. Add mixed fruit peel and spice and stir into the sandy mixture. Add the egg and enough milk to bind mixture to a rough, thick doughy texture. Using a dessertspoon, shape mixture into rough ball shapes, place on a greased baking sheet and flatten slightly. Sprinkle with demerara sugar and then bake for about 25 minutes or until firm and golden brown.

Michael Sealey

Burn O'Vat rock cakes laid out for tea in the Drawing Room at Mey

abernethy biscuits

3 oz/75g butter
8 oz/225g plain flour
3 oz/45g sugar

1 teaspoon baking powder
1 egg beaten with 1 tablespoon/15ml milk
Small teaspoon caraway seeds

Preheat the oven to 190°C/375°F/Gas 5. Rub butter into flour. Add baking powder caraway seeds and egg mixture. Turn out on to a floured board. Work to a smooth dough by hand and roll out thinly. Cut biscuits with a 3 in/7.5cm cutter. Put on a greased baking tin, prick with a fork and bake for 10 to 15 minutes. Cool on a rack before storing.

NOTE: Omit caraway seeds and turn Abernethies into Empire biscuits by sandwiching two together with a little raspberry jam. Top with glace icing and a glace cherry.

Etta Macleod

malt loaf
ease itself!

2 Weetabix
8 oz/225g mixed fruit
8 oz/225g dark brown sugar
½ pint/300ml milk
1 egg
8 oz/225g selfraising flour

Soak all the ingredients, apart from the egg and flour, in a bowl for at least 5 hours. Add the egg and flour to the mixture and mix all the ingredients together and put in 2 x 1 lb/450g loaf tins or one 2 lb/900g loaf tin. Bake in a preheated oven 180°C/350°F/Gas 4 for 1¼ hours or until a skewer inserted into centre comes out clean. This is so easy and really delicious!

Sheila Farley-Sutton

sticky gingerbread cake

A deliciously spicy sticky dark ginger cake quickly made by melting and mixing. The cake is left plain but is excellent eaten with butter or a wedge of Lancashire cheese.

8 oz /225g selfraising flour
1 teaspoon bicarbonate of soda
1 tablespoon ground ginger
1 teaspoon ground cinnamon
1 teaspoon ground mixed spice
2 grinds black pepper
4 oz/100g unsalted butter, chilled and diced

4 oz/100g black treacle
4 oz/100g golden syrup
4 oz/100g dark muscovado sugar
½ pint/300ml full cream milk
1 large free range egg, beaten to mix
(You will need one 2 lb/1kg loaf tin greased and base-lined)

Sift the flour, bicarbonate of soda, ginger, cinnamon, mixed spice and black pepper into a large mixing bowl. Add the diced butter and rub into the flour mix using the tips of your fingers until the mixture looks like breadcrumbs. Alternatively you can use a food processor and then tip the mixture into a mixing bowl. Put the treacle and golden syrup in a small pan and warm gently until melted and runny but not hot. Set aside and leave until lukewarm.

Put the sugar and milk into another pan and heat gently stirring well to dissolve the sugar. Leave to cool until lukewarm. Whisk the sweetened milk into the flour mixture quickly followed by the treacle mixture and egg to make a smooth, thick batter, the consistency of double cream. Pour the mixture into the prepared tin. Bake in a preheated oven (170°C/325°F/Gas 3) for about 45 minutes or until a skewer inserted into centre of the loaf comes out clean. Run a round-bladed knife around the inside of the tin to loosen, then set the tin on a wire rack and leave to cool completely before turning out.

Wrap in foil and leave for at least a day before cutting. It will get stickier the longer it is kept. Store in an airtight container and eat within a week.

Michael Sealey

The fireplace with copper kettle in the Equerry's Room at Mey

equerry bread

I was Equerry to Queen Elizabeth The Queen Mother between 1976 and 1978. I subsequently enjoyed fifteen summers at the Castle of Mey with Her on holiday, the last eight with my wife Rachel, so I know it well!

I am no cook, but one day I was telling Queen Elizabeth how, before I got married, I used to bake my own bread. She was fascinated and suggested that we make some that afternoon. Armed with the ingredients from the Chef, The Queen Mother and I (and Ruth Lady Fermoy, her Lady-in-Waiting) went down to the kitchen and made two loaves of bread. The kitchen was empty at the time, although I think one of the staff was there to keep an eye on us and show us where everything was. Queen Elizabeth was keen to have a go at kneading the bread. I remember Her efforts were stylish but not very productive, leaving a series of imprints in the dough of the fine pearl and diamond ring that She wore, as She rolled Her clenched fist forward, rather than kneading with the palm of Her hands!

We left the mixture to rise. It was cooked the next morning and two fine warm loaves appeared for tea on the table by the peat fire in the drawing room. Sadly Her Majesty's imprints had disappeared in the baking! I still have the simple recipe. Here it is:

1½ lb/675g strong wholemeal flour
1 tablespoon sugar
½ tablespoon of salt
½ oz/13g of butter
2 teaspoons yeast
½ pint/300ml water

Dissolve the yeast in half the water and leave for 15 minutes. Combine in a bowl the flour, sugar, salt and butter. Mix thoroughly. Add the dissolved yeast mixture with the remaining water. Knead the mixture on a flat surface and put in a warm place for several hours. Knead again briefly and put into greased baking tins. Bake in a preheated oven at 230°C/450°F/Gas 8 for 30 minutes.

I hope this works. I remember so many wonderful meals at the Castle of Mey. Incidentally, I am told that visitors are shown a painted coconut in the Library. Ashe Windham and I sent it to Her Majesty from Belize, where we were soldiering at the time, and I am amazed it has survived!

Roly Grimshaw

famous oatcakes

" This is my Grandmother's recipe, which must be over 100 years old by now. The oatcakes would be made then on an open fire with a hanging girdle and they would disappear like the proverbial 'snow off a dyke' when people visited her house on Lewis. Later they were made on a lovely old black kitchen range in Gairloch and now they are made in an Aga! We all still enjoy them so much. "

8 oz/225g medium oatmeal, plus extra to roll out
1 oz/25g plain flour
1 teaspoon sugar
Pinch salt
1 (scant) level teaspoon baking soda

1½ oz/38g margarine
1½ oz/38g fat/lard
Boiling water to mix

Break up the fat in the dry ingredients and add boiling water to make a fairly stiff but easily workable mixture. Divide and roll out (on the extra oatmeal) into rounds, then crimp the edges and sprinkle with oatmeal to give a rough texture.

Cut each round into eight sections and bake for 12 minutes in a hot preheated oven (220°C/425°F/Gas 7), top right oven in Aga. Turn the tray round once and turn oatcakes over for the last 2 minutes.

Put on cooling tray in a cool oven for 1 to 2 hours.

Catherine Mackenzie

charlie's boiled fruit cake

"Charlie Wright was a Keeper and then a Fishing Ghillie on Balmoral, and if you look in William Shawcross' biography of Queen Elizabeth, you will see that She went to tea with him during Her last visit to Birkhall. When my husband Martin Leslie retired from Balmoral and we were packing up to leave, we found a fruit cake on our doorstep which came from Charlie and was made by him, as he was a widower by then. He thought it would be useful when we arrived back on Skye! Thereafter, whenever Martin visited him he was given a cake to take home, even when he arrived with no notice!

When Charlie died, Martin was asked to speak at the funeral and, afterwards, Charlie's daughter Jane asked how she could thank him. I said that if we could have the recipe for the cake that would be a wonderful thank you so we were given it! I rang to ask her permission to use it and she said that she, on behalf of her father, would be honoured to see it in A Taste of Mey!"

15 oz/432g tin of crushed pineapple
  (discard half the juice)
12 oz/350g mixed dried fruit
8 oz/225g granulated sugar
2 eggs, whisked

4 oz/100g margarine
4 oz/100g glace cherries
1 teaspoon bicarbonate of soda
4 oz/100g self raising flour

Put crushed pineapple, margarine, mixed dried fruit, glace cherries and sugar into a saucepan and bring to the boil and simmer for 15 minutes. Remove from heat and add bicarbonate of soda and stir well. Allow to cool and then beat in the eggs, stir well, and fold in the flour. Put mixture into a greased and lined 8 in/20cm cake tin (or 2 lb/1kg loaf tin). Bake at 150°C/300°F/Gas 2 for about 1 hour and 20 mins. Leave in tin for 15 minutes and then turn out on to a rack. When cool store in an airtight tin.

Catriona Leslie

shortbread

8 oz/225g butter
4 oz/100g caster sugar, plus extra to dust
Pinch of salt

8 oz/225g plain flour
4 oz/100g fine semolina

This is my mother-in-law's recipe. Cream the butter, sugar and salt very well. Gradually add flour and semolina. Press into greased tins. Prick all over. Bake at 170°C/325°F/Gas 3 for 50 to 60 minutes. Dust with sugar. Mark out and cool slightly before cutting and putting on to a cooling rack. When quite cold put in an airtight tin.

Carol Gilmour

iced rosemary cake
unusual and delicious

3 tender fresh rosemary sprigs
  (each about 3½ in/10cm, stalks removed)
6 oz/175g unsalted butter, softened
6 oz/175g caster sugar
2 teaspoons vanilla essence
3 large eggs, beaten
8 oz/225g self-raising white flour

2 tablespoons milk

For the glaze
8 oz/225g icing sugar
Finely grated zest of ½ orange
I tablespoon orange juice
Rosemary sprigs to decorate

Grease and line a 6 in/15cm round cake tin. Finely chop the rosemary leaves and put half in a bowl with the butter and sugar. Beat until pale and creamy. Stir in the vanilla essence.Gradually beat in the eggs, a little at a time, adding a little of the flour to prevent curdling. Sift the remaining flour into the bowl. Add the milk and fold in. Turn into the prepared tin and level the surface. Bake in a preheated oven at 180°C/350°F/Gas 4 for 50 to 60 minutes or until firm and a skewer inserted into the centre comes out clean. Leave the cake to cool for 5 minutes, then run a knife between the cake and the lining paper.

Meanwhile, put the remaining chopped rosemary in a small saucepan with 2 tablespoons of water. Heat gently for 2 minutes to infuse, then leave to cool. Sift the icing sugar into a bowl and add the orange zest and juice. Strain the rosemary juice into the bowl and mix to the consistency of pouring cream, adding a little water if necessary. Pour the icing over the cake and leave to cool completely before removing paper. Decorate with rosemary sprigs to serve.

Sue Jenkins

The picnic table set sheltered against the Castle wall with not quite a Brown Betty teapot; the original now resides at Clarence House

Brown Betty

It was invariably Her Majesty Queen Elizabeth The Queen Mother's custom to take tea at 5pm wherever she was. At the Castle of Mey tea was usually served in the Drawing Room, but sometimes, if it was a warm afternoon, in 'The Dip' a well sheltered slightly sunken paved area at the south western corner of the Castle. Sometimes hampers were loaded and picnic teas were taken at places like the sunken ditch in front of the old fort at St John's Point.

At Mey visitors were regularly surprised to find the last Empress of India handing out cups of tea from a large 'Brown Betty' teapot rather than a silver or bone china pot. If their surprise was evident, Her Majesty would explain that on a train journey in the 1960s a kind station master had given it to Her when Her Majesty had admired it.

That splendid old brown teapot travelled everywhere with Her Majesty and was used in all Her residences. In fact, Her Majesty was very discerning, as connoisseurs of tea making will know that an authentic Brown Betty teapot, made of a special red clay from Bradwell Woods, first used as early as 1695, retains heat better than any comparable material.

Ashe Windham

chocolate brownies

8 oz/225g plain chocolate (70% cocoa)
8 oz/225g butter
9 oz/250g granulated sugar
3 eggs

4 oz/100g plain flour
4 oz/100g chopped walnuts or any nuts you prefer
1 teaspoon baking powder

Melt chocolate and butter in microwave or saucepan on stove. Whisk sugar and eggs together until light and fluffy. Add melted chocolate and butter to sugar and egg mixture. Finally fold in flour, nuts and baking powder to the above.

Cook in a small buttered Aga roasting pan (8 in x 12 in/20cm x 30cm) in bottom right of Aga or at 170°C/325°F/Gas 3 in a conventional oven for 30 to 35 minutes. They will be soft in the centre.

Lady Poole

Queen Elizabeth cake

" This cake was all the rage in Eastern Ontario in Coronation Year 1953 and I well remember it as a child. I hunted out the recipe and used it for a party my husband and I had to celebrate the Queen's Golden Jubilee. I also used it for a party we gave to celebrate the 100th birthday of The Queen Mother at which time our thirty-five guests were asked to wear something like The Queen Mother would wear. Our guests arrived in the most marvellous outfits, and some even came carrying pretend corgis. It was an evening to remember! "

1 oz/30g butter
5 oz/120g white sugar
1 egg (beaten)
6 oz/150g flour
1 teaspoon baking powder
¼ teaspoon salt
4 oz/100g chopped dates
1 small teaspoon bicarbonate of soda
¼ pint/240ml boiling water
2 oz/50g walnuts
1 teaspoon vanilla

For the topping
5 tablespoons brown sugar
2 oz/50g coconut
3 tablespoons butter
2 tablespoons cream

Cream the butter, then add the sugar and blend well. Add the beaten egg. Sift together the flour, baking powder and salt, and add to the first mixture. Pour boiling water over the dates and bicarbonate of soda and let them soak for a few minutes. Drain and then add to the above. Stir in walnuts and vanilla. Bake for 30 minutes at 180°C/350°F/Gas 4. Allow to cool slightly.

For the topping, boil the ingredients for 3 minutes, stirring continuously. Pour over the warm, baked cake, then return to the oven and brown under the grill.

Sarah Jane Drumbrille

welsh teabread

" This is the recipe we use for HRH The Duke of Rothesay's afternoon teabread. "

1 mug of sultanas
1 mug of raisins
A large pinch of mixed peel, finely chopped
1 mug of soft brown sugar

1 mug of strong Earl Grey or smoked black tea
1 egg, beaten
1½ mugs of self-raising flour

Mix the fruit, peel and sugar in a large bowl. Pour the mug of strong Earl Grey or smoked black tea over the mixture. Leave to soak for a few hours. Mix well and fold in the beaten egg. Fold in enough selfraising flour to make a soft batter (this will be about 1½ mugs).

Bake in a loaf tin, at 150°C/300°F/Gas 2 for just over 1 hour.

Julian Williams

Queen Elizabeth's staff split into two teams to cover the duration of Her Majesty's stay in Scotland. It was hard work so we welcomed the long relaxing train journey back home down south. A group of us were travelling together on the train, a couple of chefs, footmen, a dresser, a porter and William Tallon (the Page). We boarded the train and settled down in our seats for a journey that would take several hours. After a while William Tallon became bored and declared he would love one of his cousin's ginger cookies: "Naomi makes really good ginger cookies". We didn't think that was much use to us stuck on a train, but William assured us that Naomi would either have some or be able to make some. "This train goes through Newcastle Station, I'll get her to bring some when we stop there". So that's exactly what happened. William phoned his cousin and told her the train would call at Newcastle in a couple of hours, which gave her the time to make us a fresh batch of biscuits if she had to. When we got to Newcastle, a volunteer footman was despatched to run the length of the platform until he came across an attractive young girl carrying a biscuit tin. It was like a scene from a film! The footman raced back onto the train but needn't have worried as the guard held the train for him. When the guard found out who we worked for she kindly said that we could move up to First Class! You see it's not always a case of what you know...

Bruce Guest

Going south the old-fashioned way!

naomi's ginger biscuits

" *I am delighted to share this recipe for my famous ginger biscuits!* *"*

8 oz/225g self raising flour
4 oz/100g golden syrup
4 oz/100g margarine
2 oz/50g caster sugar
1½ teaspoons of bicarbonate of soda
4-5 teaspoons of ground ginger (to taste)
1 teaspoon mixed spice
½ teaspoon cinnamon
Pinch of salt

Melt the syrup, margarine and sugar in a pan over a low heat until the sugar has dissolved. Blend all the dried ingredients into the mixture. Stir well and then allow to cool.

Divide the mixture into walnut-sized balls and roll out, placing on to a greased baking tray.

Bake at 170°C/325°F/Gas 3 for 10 to 15 minutes.

Naomi Featherstone
William Tallon's first cousin

sheila's fruit loaf

" *This recipe never fails and is a favourite with my family and friends. My great grandfather George Heggie was head gardener at the Castle from 1870-1913, when he died. My Granny Georgina Heggie was brought up in the Castle.* "

4 oz/100g margarine
10 floz/240 ml water
4 oz/100g sugar white or brown
8 oz/225g mixed fruit

½ teaspoon of baking soda
8 oz/225g self raising flour
2 beaten eggs

Put all ingredients except flour and eggs into a pan and simmer for 20 minutes. Cool slightly before gradually adding flour and eggs. Beat all together. Turn out into a loaf tin which has been lined with greaseproof paper and bake for ¾ hr at 170°C/325°F/Gas 3. Test cake in the middle with a skewer which should come out clean if the loaf is cooked.

Sheila Heggie Main

sherry and almond cake

7 oz/200g self-raising flour
almond essence
4 eggs
2 tablespoons sherry
2 oz/50g ground almonds

8 oz/225g caster sugar
8 oz/225g butter or margarine
A few blanched almonds
Pinch of salt

Grease and line a square or round cake tin (7 in/17.5cm or 8 in/20cm diameter). Sieve together flour, salt and ground almonds. Cream together butter and sugar until white and fluffy.

Add beaten eggs one at a time. Add the flour mixture gradually folding it in lightly. Lastly, stir in sherry and a few drops almond essence. Put in prepared tin, smooth level, scatter top with split blanched almonds. Bake in a moderate oven for an hour then lower heat for a further hour or until cake is cooked through and a good golden colour.

The Dowager Countess of Strathmore
Recipe courtesy of Mrs Veronica Goodall, Glamis Castle Cook for many years

mrs murray's ginger sponge

"The Murray family were farmers at Sibster, four miles from Wick. Their lovely daughter Nellie had her own hairdressing salon in Tolbooth Lane, Wick, right opposite my parents' home. She became my mother's best friend. When my parents married in 1940 they returned home to Wick by train (not on that occasion driven by my father!) and Mrs Murray waved a huge white tablecloth from her front door to welcome the newly married couple. As a child in later years I remember looking out for Mrs Murray and her tablecloth each time we journeyed by train. This recipe was given to my Mum by Mrs Murray and is in Mum's old recipe book as "Mrs Murray's Ginger Sponge". It must be well over 100 years old and is still in use – and remains very popular. It is a constant reminder of three generations of fond friendship."

8 oz/225g plain flour
2 oz/50g margarine
2 tablespoons syrup
¾ teaspoon baking soda
½ teaspoon cream of tartar

4 oz/100g sugar
½ cup milk
1 egg
1 teaspoon ginger
1 teaspoon mixed spice

Melt together the sugar, milk, margarine and syrup in a pan. Sift dry ingredients and beat egg. Add to melted mixture. Put into 2 sandwich tins and bake on top shelf at 190°C/375°F/Gas 5 for 20 to 25 minutes or until firm and a skewer inserted into the centre comes out clean. Add a butter icing filling or topping.

Anne Dunnett

Tea in the Drawing Room in the
Castle with its new carpet

The Drawing Room Carpet

I pestered The Queen Mother to get a new carpet in the Drawing Room for over 20 years. Eventually one day She called me into the Drawing Room to tell me that we were at last going to get a new one, as HM The Queen was giving it to Her for her 90th Birthday. The interior designer at Clarence House, Oliver Ford, was to organise it. To start with we had to take up the old carpet which had been there from before The Queen Mother bought the Castle of Mey, and I managed to fit it into a tatty bag to be taken to Mackays of Bradford to make a replica. Because it was to be made in an old style, Mackays used an old loom to make it and brought a man out of retirement to make it. He came up with the carpet fitters to oversee it being installed and when The Queen Mother heard his story She wrote to him to thank him. He was so delighted.

June Webster

june's oatcakes

8 oz/225g medium oatmeal
4 oz/100g self raising flour, sifted
½ teaspoon bicarbonate of soda
Pinch of salt
4 oz/100g Parmesan cheese
1 dessertspoon chopped rosemary
Water, to mix
5 oz/125g butter

Mix the flour, bicarbonate and oatmeal in a bowl. Rub in butter. Add cheese, rosemary and salt. Add a little water at a time to make a manageable dough. Roll out fairly thin and cut out as preferred. Bake at 170°C/325°F/Gas 3. Watch carefully as they burn easily. My tip is to flour the tray sparingly. Cool and store in an airtight tin. Very nice!

June Webster

A Breach of Protocol?

It was the morning of Queen Elizabeth's 100th birthday and I was waiting at the bottom of the stairs to wish Her happy birthday. About two steps from the bottom of the staircase She stopped and enquired, "Why are there so many people outside the gates this morning?" I explained that it was Her 100th birthday and the nation was very excited. She negotiated the last two steps, stopped at the bottom and said, "That's very nice, but it's just another birthday." With that She strode off down the corridor to deal with the daily correspondence, as She did every morning, with the accompanying tea and biscuits.

As She did every year, Her Majesty would appear at the gates of Clarence House to receive birthday greetings and presents from the assembled well wishers. This year was obviously very special as it was Her 100th, and a telegram from The Queen was due to be delivered by the Palace postman. The red post van duly arrived and the gathered media across the road started clicking away as the telegram was presented. The crowd cheered and sang Happy Birthday. Her Majesty received the telegram and with The Prince of Wales standing behind Her She proceeded to open it. Either the fingers were not as nimble as they used to be or more likely The Queen had firmly sealed the envelope, but Her Majesty appeared to struggle a little to open it. Prince Charles noticed this and indicated that my sword might be a suitable letter opener, so I enquired if my sword could be of service for opening the telegram! Quick as a flash Her Majesty, who always enjoyed some fun and ceremony, said that was a splendid idea. I duly drew my sword and sliced open the envelope, to allow Her Majesty to open and read the telegram. As this happened there was a gasp from some of the onlookers and the press started clicking furiously.

It was only when we all returned into Clarence House that various people commented on the potential breach of 'protocol' to draw one's sword in front of a Monarch! Was it an act of treason? Finally, as we sat down to lunch that day, Captain Mark Grayson, who was about to succeed me as Equerry, commented that if I was on the front of the evening paper he would stab me with his pen, with which the Orderly walked in with the evening paper and the front page full of the telegram opening incident!

William de Rouet

Opening Her Majesty's 100th birthday telegram

gooey chocolate cake

8 oz/225g butter
8 oz/225g sugar
5 eggs separated
1 tablespoon orange marmalade
5 oz/125g cooking chocolate
8 oz/225g plain flour
2 teaspoons baking powder
2 oz/50g sweet ground almonds

For the chocolate butter icing
¼ lb/100g plain unsweetened solid chocolate
½ lb/225g icing sugar
4 oz/100g butter softened
1 egg beaten
A few drops each of vanilla and almond essence

Preheat oven to 170°C/325°F/Gas 3.

Beat butter and sugar to a light cream. Add egg yolks and marmalade. Stir in chocolate, previously melted over a low heat. Add flour, baking powder and almonds.

Whip egg whites and fold in lightly. Pour into a greased 8 in/20cm cake tin and bake in oven for 1 hour and 15 minutes. When cool cut into three layers.

To make the icing, melt chocolate over a low heat. Sieve icing sugar into a bowl, stir in the softened butter, add chocolate and beaten egg and stir until smooth and light. Add flavouring and spread immediately between layers of chocolate cake and on top with a palette knife. Some of the icing can be piped on top with a forcing bag.

Taken from 'To Set Before a Queen: The Royal Cookery of Mrs McKee' (Gracewing Publishing).
This recipe appears under the menu for a Tennis Party and it might well have been the cake
Mrs McKee always made for Queen Elizabeth The Queen Mother's birthday.

bishop's bread

12 oz/325g dark brown sugar
20 oz/550g sifted all-purpose flour
½ teaspoon salt
2 teaspoon baking powder
2 teaspoon cinnamon

40 oz/100g lard
1 egg, beaten
15 floz/360ml cups buttermilk
1½ teaspoons baking soda

Sift the first five ingredients together 3 times. Mix in shortening. Set aside 6 oz/175g of the above for topping later. Mix soda into buttermilk and add. Stir in beaten egg. Pour into two 8-inch buttered cake pans. Spread the reserved crumbly mixture over the top. Bake at 180°C/350°F/Gas 4 for 20 to 25 minutes. Serve immediately. Delicious with tea.

St Swithun's Society, Ontario

" I have visited our Archives files and have been looking through our collection of items related to Her Late Majesty, Queen Elizabeth the Queen Mother. At our Celebrations on St. Swithun's Day 1998, I remember telling our membership that I had received the most gracious and beautiful rejection slip ever after our suggestion of the name "Swithun" for Her Majesty's new foal.

With renewed good wishes,
Norman McMullen KStG
President, St. Swithun's Society **"**

CLARENCE HOUSE
S.W.1

3rd April 1998

Dear Mr. McMullen,

I have been asked by Queen Elizabeth The Queen Mother to thank you and all who joined with you for your latest letter, and all the good wishes you sent to Her Majesty.

I am to say that The Queen Mother was so pleased that it proved possible for her to attend race meetings at both Sandown Park and Cheltenham recently.

I am also to let you know that at present a name has not yet been officially selected for the foal born earlier this year, but I am afraid that your kind suggestion is not among those still being considered.

Yours sincerely,

Margaret Colville

Lady-in-Waiting

Mr. N. McMullen.

Castle of Mey Christmas Cake

A tradition of presenting a Christmas cake to the local primary school at Mey was started in 1929 by the Imbert-Terrys, the then owners of the Castle of Mey, which the The Queen Mother carried on. Following Her Majesty's death, HRH The Prince Charles, Duke of Rothesay has continued the practice, much to the delight of staff and pupils. Making it is an annual team effort at the Castle.

(You will need an 8 in/20cm square or 9 in/23cm round cake tin, a 10 in/25.5cm square or 11in/28cm round cake board)

13 oz/375g raisins
10 oz/275g sultanas
8 oz/225g currants
6 oz/175g glacé cherries, halved
3 oz/75g mixed peel (in blender with
   1 tablespoon flour)
4 oz/125g ground almonds
2½ teaspoon lemon rind
2½ tablespoon lemon juice
4 tablespoon brandy/sherry

11 oz/325g plain flour
1 tablespoon mixed spice
9 oz/250g soft light dark brown or caster sugar
9 oz/250g butter, softened
5 eggs, beaten

For the icing
Apricot jam, for glaze
2 lb/900g marzipan
2 lb/900g/ fondant icing

Oven (preheat) 140°C/275°F/Gas 1. Line cake tin with 2 or 3 layers of bakewell or greaseproof paper. Around the outside of the tin, tie 2 or 3 layers of brown paper with string and line a baking sheet with 3 or 4 layers of brown paper. Stand cake tin on top in oven. Also have a sheet of brown paper to cover top of the tin.

Wash raisins sultanas and currants. Put all in a sieve and pour over some slightly cooled boiled water, then dry immediately and put into large bowl. Repeat with cherries. Add other fruit and almonds, finally adding fruit juice, brandy or sherry and leave to soak overnight.

Sift the flour and spices together. Cream the butter and sugar until light and fluffy and add some beaten egg and flour mixture to this mixture taking care it does not curdle. Continue adding egg and flour together until all dry ingredients are used up. Gradually add the soaked fruit mixture and fold into cake mixture using a wooden spoon until everything is evenly blended.

Spoon mixture into the prepared tin, spreading evenly and giving container a few sharp bangs to level mixture and remove any air bubbles. Smooth the surface with the back of a metal spoon, making a slight depression in the centre. Bake in the centre of the oven for approximately 3 to 3 ¾ hours. After first hour cover top with the folded paper. Check cooking at 3 hours. The cake should be firm and when a fine cake skewer is inserted into the centre it should come out quite clean. If the cake is not cooked retest at 15-minute intervals.

Remove cake from oven and allow to cool in tin. When cold, turn cake out of the tin but do not remove the lining paper as it helps to keep the moisture in. The addition of brandy/sherry can be done before the cake is overwrapped in greaseproof and then tin foil for storage. Store in a cool dry place until ready to marzipan and ice.

To ice, unwrap cake, brush top with apricot jam to glaze. Knead the marzipan on a surface lightly dusted with icing sugar and roll out a sheet approximately ¼ inch/0.6cm thick to cover top and sides of cake. Carefully apply to cake using smoothers. Leave covered with greaseproof paper for a few days to set. Brush top of marzipan on the cake with cooled boiled water or vodka. Prepare fondant icing in same way as marzipan and apply to the cake.

Complete in desired decoration.

Helen Malcolm

hoosh-mi *

* Hoosh-mi was a word devised by HRH The Princess Margaret which became part of schoolroom vocabulary to describe a mix of any kind.

The drinks table in the Drawing Room at Mey

lemon curd

Grated rind and juice of 4 lemons
4 eggs, beaten
4 oz/100g butter
1 lb/450g granulated sugar

Put all ingredients into a bowl and stand in pan of simmering water. Continue heating, stirring occasionally, until sugar has dissolved and curd thickens. Pot into small jars and store in the fridge. Use within one month.

Gwen Coghill

damson jam

"Her Majesty was frequently given various homemade fruit gins by Ladies and Gentlemen visiting the Castle. I was privileged to do the tipple test, and duly collected the recipes. Having bottled the gin, what to do with all the gorgeous gin-infused fruit? We make ours into jam!"

Weigh your fruit and place in a large thick bottomed pan. Make life easy and buy preserving sugar; the ratio is on the packet. Simply boil together gently until a little cooled on plate begins to set. Remove from the heat and cool slightly before using a ladle to rub it through a sieve to rid the stones, then put into clean warm jars. Enjoy on toast or with rice pudding.

Sue Collings

gooseberry jelly

Wash the gooseberries. Cover them with cold water in a preserving pan. Bring to the boil and simmer until the fruit is reduced to pulp. Leave overnight to strain through a jelly bag. For every pint/600ml of juice allow 1 lb/450g of sugar. Boil up the juice and sugar for about 10 minutes and test for setting.

Christine Shearer

rosemary jelly

We love this delicious homemade golden rosemary jelly, which is great with game but especially good with lamb or mutton.

8 lb/3.6kg Bramley cooking apples
1 large handful of rosemary leaves
   washed and stripped from the stalks

1½ pints/900ml of water
½ pint/300ml white wine vinegar
1 lb/450g granulated sugar per pint of liquids

Cut up the whole unpeeled apples into ½ inch cubes and add to a large jam-making pan. Add the water and half the rosemary leaves and bring to the boil, stirring regularly. Reduce to a simmer for about 40 minutes or until very soft. Add the vinegar and bring back to a simmer for a further 10 minutes.

Allow to cool. Pour contents into a jelly bag supported over a large pan and strain for about 12 hours – overnight is a good idea. Measure the extracted juice and place back into the pan adding 1 lb/450g of granulated sugar for each pint of juice. Bring to a rapid boil for about 10 minutes or until setting point is reached. Add the remainder of the rosemary leaves, stir and pour into warmed jam jars.

Mike Palmer and Clive Illingworth

poached quinces

4 fresh quinces
Dry red wine

Small jar of honey
4 cinnamon sticks

Peel the quinces but leave the fruit whole and, if possible, leave the stalk on the fruit. Place them upright in a saucepan. Cover completely with the dry red wine. Add the honey and cinnamon sticks to the saucepan. Bring to the boil and lower heat to simmer for approximately 45 minutes. Test to see if the fruit is cooked with a sharp knife or skewer. Remove the cooked fruit and put to one side. Reduce the wine and honey until a coulis consistency is reached. Place the fruit in a serving dish, cover with the coulis and serve with vanilla ice cream.

Lili Panagi

"Is that who I think it is?!"

Quite often Queen Elizabeth came for a 'picnic' at the Captain's House, which is next door to the Castle of Mey and where I lived and worked for a fortnight or so each August while at Mey. In the early days the chauffeur would arrive at 11.30am and take my typing table, which left me typing on the floor, but in latter days another table was provided. On wet days Her Majesty had Her picnic in the little sitting room (this was of course before the conservatory was added). On fine days She was in the front garden.

Quite often tourist buses paused outside the cottage while the guide told them about Her Majesty and the Castle. This obviously amused Queen Elizabeth and more than once She raised Her glass to whoever in the coach was looking away from the castle towards Captain's House. This of course had the effect of making the coach rock considerably as the bemused tourists rushed to see if it really was Her Majesty and take photos!

Fiona Fletcher

Opposite: The Captain's House with the added conservatory, as viewed from the top of the tower of the Castle of Mey

bure house original marmalade

This recipe has been used by my family for at least three generations. It was taught to me by my mother, and I have only once or twice had a failure. Quite good, I think, as I am a bachelor, and a very mediocre cook! We keep a Marmalade Book for fun, in which is recorded any change to the recipe, quantities of fruit and sugar used as well as the all important 'yield'. Also, I have recorded as we say in Norfolk, "for curio", anything special that happened on that day.

January 15th 1994

A frantic day, nothing going right, burst the pip bag while boiling. Just before the marmalade setting, another telephone call. I answered it abruptly, telling them to be quick because I was making marmalade, only to discover it was the Lady-in-Waiting from Sandringham with an invitation from Queen Elizabeth to dinner! I am thankful to say that no offence was taken and I gave Her Majesty a jar of the marmalade. This continued for each following year and I am told it was made into a marmalade pudding of which She was very fond.

January 26th 2005

Disaster! All ditched! What a waste!! Satsumas used instead of Seville oranges!

February 1st 2007

Farewell to the Royal Green Jackets, Hello to The Rifles. My Godson is now Colonel Commandant of The Rifles which was formed today.

---

3 lb/1.35g Seville oranges   1 grapefruit or sweet orange
3 lemons   6 pints/3.6ltr of water
Sugar

Boil the fruit for about an hour or until the liquid has reduced by about half. Carefully remove the fruit and, when cooled, cut into quarters. Remove pips and stringy pith and place on a piece of muslin which can be tied up and used as a 'pip bag'. Cut the peel into any required size (I cut it as thin as possible) and put with the fruit pulp and water into a preserving pan.

NOTE: Remember to weigh the pan when empty, as you will have to deduct this weight from when it is full before cooking.

Add 1 lb/450g of sugar to every pint/600 ml of pulp and liquid. Tie the 'pip bag' to the handle of the pan so that it is covered by the pulp to help the setting process. Boil HARD for 8 minutes and then test. I put a small amount on to a saucer and put it into the fridge to cool quicker. As soon as it has 'wrinkled' it is set. Pour into warmed jars when cool enough, and place tops on when the marmalade is cold. (See also marmalade pudding recipe on page 150.)

Johnnie Perkins

Johnnie Perkins is now keeping hens and has one called 'Marmalade'!

nana swanson's beetroot chutney

" It was my wedding on 31 July 2009 that was the first to take place at the Castle of Mey in recent times. It was an appropriate venue for me, as I have strong family links with the Castle. My late grandfather was born in the Gardener's Cottage and many of the family worked there, then at Barrogill Castle. The last wedding to take place at the Castle before mine was that of my great, great aunt in 1904. "

3 lbs/1.5 kg beetroot, stalks removed
1½ lbs/675g cooking apples, peeled and chopped
½ lb/225g sugar
2 large onions, chopped
1 pint/600ml vinegar
½ teaspoon ginger

Boil the beetroot for one hour. Drain and allow to cool, then peel and dice. Place the vinegar in saucepan, then add the sugar, ginger, apples and onions and boil for 20 minutes. Add the beetroot cubes and boil for 15 minutes. Allow to cool, then place into jars.

Susan MacColl

rhubarb chutney

2 lb/1kg rhubarb stalks
2 lb/1kg brown sugar
2 onions
1 oz/25g salt
½ teaspoon cayenne pepper
2 lemons
1 oz/25g ground ginger
1 pint/600ml vinegar
1 lb/450g sultanas

Cut the rhubarb into small pieces. Remove skin from lemons and take out pips. Cut onion into small pieces. Put all the ingredients into a pan and boil at a moderate pace for about an hour until it thickens. Stir frequently. When cold pour into jars and cover.

This recipe was used by my mother, the late Mrs Christian Bell, the wife of the Minister at Canisbay Kirk, and is probably the 'pickles' referred to in The Queen Mother's letter [pictured opposite].

Christine Shearer

By Hand

Mrs Bell
Mey

August 22nd
1982

ER

Castle of Mey

Dear Mrs Bell

It was so very
kind of you to send over
those lovely pots of jam
& pickles, and we have
all been enjoying the
contents enormously.
The rhubarb is a

great success, and I
am so grateful to you
for giving me such a
toothsome gift.
With my warm thanks,
I am yours very sincerely
Elizabeth R

PM Lard Melvilles

Very thin rashers of streaky bacon. Dip in beaten egg and white breadcrumbs (this can be done in advance). Cook under grill or in a very hot oven. They can also be fried in deep fat. They keep crisp in a cool oven. Good as a savoury.

(from Christina Murray)

Henry Gillespie's
After Eight ice cream

2 boxes of 'After Eight' choc mints
2 oz caster sugar
6 egg yolks
10 oz double cream
125ml wineglass of brandy

Boil sugar in 8 fluid oz water for 3 minutes. Put in blender with mints and blend until melted. Add beaten egg yolks and blend for 15 seconds. Leave in blender to cool. Add brandy and cream and blend for 10 seconds. Pour into dishes/glasses and freeze.

Lemon Sweet

(from Jane Walker-Okeover)

1 large tub Greek yoghurt
Juice and rind of 1 lemon
6 tablespoons of lemon curd

Mix and leave in the fridge to set. Quick and simple and looks good in little individual glasses or dishes!

Christine Shearer's Sandwich Spread

Process together a tin of lean corned beef, 3 hard boiled eggs, 2 skinned tomatoes, 1/4 lb butter, a dessertspoon chutney, teaspoon chopped onion, a few drops Lea & Perrins sauce and salt and pepper to taste.

Little Haggis Pots

Bash up a haggis and sprinkle with whisky. Divide into 4 or 6 ramekins and cover with onion sauce. Top with clapshot, i.e. tatties and turnip mashed together. Bake.

(My own creation, which is such an easy starter and one of my favourites. Also good for lunchtime in one dish. My son Patrick used to cook this at Kylesku Hotel in Sutherland probably minus the whisky!)
– Lady Gilmour

Very simple choc mousse

2 oz plain choc
2 eggs, separated

Melt the chocolate carefully in a bowl over hot water. When cooler stir in the eggs. Beat white until stiff and fold into mixture. Place in fridge to set. Decorate with grated chocolate or piped whipped cream. In the summer decorate with raspberries. These are good served in individual glasses.

(Jane Walker-Okeover's recipe)

Don't forget to feed the corgis!

Lamb Piquant
(Catriona Leslie's amazing sauce)

3 tablespoons butter
2 tablespoons tomato ketchup
1 tablespoon vinegar
3 tablespoons (or less) redcurrant jelly

Mix all the ingredients together and pour over finely sliced cold lamb. Heat in a covered dish and serve with potatoes and a vegetable or a salad. I also add raisins as an optional extra.

Royal Picnics

Queen Elizabeth thoroughly enjoyed alfresco picnic lunches and had several favourite places near the Castle of Mey. Walled cemeteries, which dotted the Caithness landscape, provided a perfect windbreak and, on rare occasions, a suntrap for these picnics.

During the morning the picnic would be set up by Her Page, William Tallon, and the house party would assemble for lunch in the cemetery if they had been fishing on the River Thurso or walking up grouse near Mey. Drinks were served, and come rain or shine Queen Elizabeth and Her guests would sit on picnic chairs round a couple of somewhat wobbly tables. The picnic usually included Oeufs Drumkilbo (a combination of hard-boiled eggs, tomatoes, lobster, prawns, fresh mayonnaise, white wine and a considerable amount of cream). After lunch Queen Elizabeth would encourage the party to set out across the moors to walk off their lunch.

Richard Jenkins

PICNIC AT CAMERON'S COTTAGE

Royal Salutes

In the summer it was customary for HM The Queen to visit the Castle of Mey during Her annual holiday aboard *HMY Britannia*. The Queen and Her guests would disembark from the Royal Yacht at Scrabster nearby and would be driven to the Castle for lunch.

Later in the day The Queen would re-embark and *Britannia* and her Royal Navy escort ship would sail slowly past the Castle of Mey through the Pentland Firth. Queen Elizabeth would wave to *Britannia* from a clifftop near the Castle and the local coastguards would let off flares and maroons by way of a Royal Salute.

Richard Jenkins

These photographs were taken by Captain Richard Jenkins when on a visit to Mey in 1968-69 when he was an Equerry to Queen Elizabeth.

Opposite above (from the left around the table): Lady Doris Vyner; Ruth, Lady Fermoy (partly hidden); HM; Comdr Clare Vyner RN; Captain David McMicking

Opposite below (from the left): HM; Comdr Clare Vyner RN; Sir Martin Gilliatt; Lady Doris Vyner; Captain David McMicking; Ruth, Lady Fermoy; Captain Richard Jenkins (centre)

This page: *HMY Britannia* sailing past Mey with the local coastguards setting off flares and maroons in salute to HM The Queen who had earlier lunched at Mey.

bloody bull

" This cocktail was served at a luncheon I attended hosted by the Tasmanian-born Dorothy Hammerstein, widow of Oscar Hammerstein II, at 550 Park Avenue, New York, on 10th December 1981. Prior to luncheon, guests were offered one of Dorothy's special cocktails, a 'Bloody Bull'. She had been given the recipe by musical comedy star Adele Astaire (sister of Fred Astaire) who married Lord Charles Cavendish, brother of the tenth Duke of Devonshire. As Dorothy shook the cocktail shaker, she told me that Noël Coward had asked for the recipe and offered Queen Elizabeth The Queen Mother one when she visited him in Jamaica on 28th February 1965. The Queen Mother paused for a second and said, "Delicious... just the thing to get us going!" "

SERVES 2
1 small tin beef consommé
Same amount of tomato juice
2 tablespoons vodka
Generous amount Worcester sauce
1 teaspoon dill weed

Combine all of the ingredients in the shaker with plenty of ice. Shake well and serve.

I am a retired barrister and have been an arts advocate and patron in Australia and New York, USA, for over 30 years. I was first presented to Queen Elizabeth The Queen Mother at Clarence House on 24th November 1981. Her Majesty told me of her first visit to Australia as Duchess of York. The Duke of York had been invited to open the new Parliament House in the nation's capital, Canberra, on 9th May 1927. They travelled by train from Melbourne and Queen Elizabeth wore a white dress which quickly turned red because of the dust.

From 1980 to 1987 I was Australian editor of Andy Warhol's Interview *magazine and am one of only two Australians to have been painted by Warhol. Andy Warhol was a great admirer of Queen Elizabeth, and had Cecil Beaton photographs of her and souvenir biscuit tins, with photos of the Royal Family on the lids, displayed in bookcases at The Factory, New York.*

I was invited to stay at the Castle of Mey but unfortunately I was never able to be in Scotland at the right time. I have many happy memories of Queen Elizabeth The Queen Mother, whose generosity of spirit has left an indelible mark.

Henry Gillespie

elderflower cordial

20 elderflower heads, picked in the sun
Juice of 2 lemons
2 lb/1kg sugar
2 oz/50g citric acid (health shops have it)
3 pints/1.8l of boiling water

Put first four ingredients in a bowl and pour on the boiling water, stirring until the sugar dissolves.

Leave for 24 hours and then strain. Dilute to taste. This cordial does not keep long in the fridge but freezes well. I put it in ½ pint/300ml cream cartons that have plastic lids.

Depending on where the elderflowers are growing and what the weather is like, they are out between May and July.

Jane Walker-Okeover

215

Something in the Water...

When I was a guide in the pantry at Mey in 2010, I had a little running list of what to say to the visitors. I told this little tale and everyone seemed to like it. I was a bit reticent at first, thinking that it may be too much information, but decided that it helped in playing down Queen Elizabeth's reputation as being wholly extravagant. Anyway, here is the little tale...

The main duty of the footmen was to serve meals and drinks. When we laid a table we would always fill the water glasses. We would then top up the glasses during the meal using bottles of Malvern (English mineral water). At the Castle of Mey, we were told (by William, the Page) to fill the bottles up with tap water "as it's such a shame not to use the lovely Scottish water, as it's so good for you." Nobody seemed to notice, I mean mind, so that was that. We didn't do this when we were at Balmoral though, as the soft, peaty water there is ever so slightly coloured and it would have given the game away. Wonderful bathing water though!

This is just one example of frugalness, as we were working in an environment that was influenced by wartime austerity. We were using certain pieces of equipment that were years old and definitely out of fashion but still worked perfectly, so why change them?

This, I think, also has something to do with the fact that quality lasts. A little Champagne every night was not such a bad idea after all.

Above: Caithness glass at Mey

Bruce Guest

orkney bride's cog for 100 guests

> *A Cog is a wooden drinking vessel used at Orkney wedding feasts and the bride has to be the first to drink out of the Bride's Cog before it is passed round to everyone present.*

15 bottles ale
½ bottle rum
3 bottles strong ale
1½ bottles whisky
½ bottle port

1½ tablespoons ground ginger
1½ tablespoons cloves
1½ tablespoons ground black pepper
1½ tablespoons nutmeg
3 cups brown sugar

Put all the ingredients into a very large pot and bring to the boil. Cool slightly before putting into the Bride's Cog and serving. There are variations of the above but all are worthwhile!

Hamish Pottinger

nana miller's tablet

2 lb/1kg sugar
Small tin sweetened condensed milk
¼ lb/100g butter
½ pint/300ml milk and water mixed

Mix together the sugar, milk and water. Bring to the boil and add the butter. When the mixture is sticky add the condensed milk. Boil until the mixture gets sugary. Beat.

Hazel Farquhar
Nana Miller was Hazel's mother. Hazel and her family still live in Mey and her daughter is Shirley Farquhar, who had the idea for this book.

If during dinner there was a renowned north-coast sunset, The Queen Mother would usher Her guests into the Butler's Pantry adjacent to the Dining Room, from where they could look out over the Castle's walled garden and watch the sun setting over Dunnet Head.

weights and measures

oven temperatures

°C	°F	Gas Mark	°C	°F	Gas Mark
110	225	¼	190	375	5
130	250	½	200	400	6
140	275	1	220	425	7
150	300	2	230	450	8
170	325	3	240	475	9
180	350	4			

spoon measures

1 teaspoon	=	5ml
4 teaspoons	=	1 tablespoon
1 tablespoon	=	20ml (approx.)
1 rounded spoon	=	2 level spoons

american conversions

	US	UK	METRIC
Butter / sugar	2 tbsp	1 oz	25g
	¼ cup	2 oz	50g
	½ cup	4 oz	100g
	¾ cup	6 oz	175g
	1 cup	8 oz	225g
Flour	¼ cup	1 oz	25g
	½ cup	2 oz	50g
	¾ cup	3 oz	75g
	1 cup	4 oz	100g
Icing sugar / cocoa / cornflour	1 cup	4½ oz	120g
Liquids / cream / yogurt	¼ cup	2½ floz	60ml
	½ cup	5 floz	120ml
	¾ cup	7½ floz	180ml
	1 cup	10 fl oz	240ml
	1 pt (2 cups)	20 fl oz	480ml
Rice	1 cup	8 oz	230g
Grated cheese / chopped nuts	1 cup	4 oz	100g
Yeast	1 cake, pkg	4 oz fresh	15g

metric conversions*

SOLIDS

IMPERIAL	METRIC
1 oz	25g
2 oz	50g
4 oz	100g
8 oz	225g
12 oz	350g
14 oz	400g
1 lb (16 oz)	450g
2.2 lb	1kg

LIQUIDS

IMPERIAL	METRIC
¼ pint	150ml
½ pint	300ml
1 pint	600ml
1½ pints	900ml
1¾ pints	1 litre

*whilst not exact conversions, these are recommended conversion quantities

food ounce to spoon conversions

FOOD	LEVEL SPOONS TO 1 OZ (25g)
Butter	2 tablespoons
Sugar	2 tablespoons
Flour / cornflour	2 tablespoons
Syrup / treacle / honey	1 tablespoon
Fresh bread or cake crumbs	4 tablespoons
Rice	2 tablespoons
Rolled oats	3 tablespoons
Sultanas, raisins, currants	2 tablespoons
Gelatine	3 tablespoons

contents index

Photography by Iain MacLeod-Jones. Additional photography of the gardens at the Castle of Mey by Shirley Farquhar and Olga Ridley. Original drawing on page 117 by Sarah Walford. Photograph on page 10 by Tim Graham; photograph on page 17 by Julia Boardman; photographs on pages 40, 212, 213 by Captain Richard Jenkins; photographs on pages 70, 81, 132, 160 by Mrs Janet McDonald of McDonald Photographers, Wick; photographs on pages 136, 137, 141 from the archive at the Castle of Mey; photograph on page 118 by Jack Spellingbacon; photograph on page 149 by Matt Riggott; photograph on page 167 by Stanislav Kozlovskiy; photograph on page 195 © Telegraph Media Group Limited 2000 / Ian Jones (through the generosity of William de Rouet); photograph on page 199 by Ian Malcolm. Additional images on pages 33, 39, 43, 47, 62, 63, 64, 66, 68-70, 78, 79, 84, 88, 89, 93, 95, 102, 106, 107, 109, 111, 113, 114, 122, 123, 126, 127, 134, 135, 142, 149, 154, 163, 165, 177, 181, 186-189, 196, 202, 203, 207, 208, 210, 211, 214, 215, 221 courtesy of www.canstockphoto.com, © Can Stock Photo Inc.

www.imjdesign.co.uk